Know Yourself!

**When you take care of *yourself*,
everyone around you benefits.**

Nancy Howes, Founder, Know Yourself, Inc.

Dr. Bonyfide PRESENTS

For ages 6 to 206!

BONES OF THE HAND, ARM, AND SHOULDER **BOOK 1**

A *KNOW YOURSELF, INC.* CREATION
SAN FRANCISCO, CALIFORNIA

Created by Know Yourself, Inc.

Copyright ©2014 Know Yourself, Inc. All rights reserved.
www.knowyourself.com

Cover and Interior Design: Derek Bacchus

ISBN 978-0-9912968-0-4
Library of Congress Control Number: 2014939890
Printed in the United States of America

Who in the world am I? Ah, that is the great puzzle.

Lewis Carroll

Acknowledgements

Thanks to Tim, Zhi, and Maddy for listening and for looking at all the materials with unwavering enthusiasm, love, and honest feedback.

Bonnie O'Connell, Linda Balfour, and Anne MacKenzie for their steadfast willingness to give their time and years of expertise to help make this an enjoyable process for the kids.

Dan McKernan for encouraging Joanie to jump in the deep end on this project. Her participation was essential to its success.

We are indebted to Michael Penne, our publishing mentor, for his expertise, good humor, unending network of resources, and continual support on this project.

Lidie Howes, Whitney Noble, and Helen Heaslip for their editing help and love of the English language and its rules. We took some liberties, but I think you all helped us color in the lines.

Derek Bacchus who helped us reach for the gold standard. Thank you for your grace.

Marni Martens, who shared her valuable opinions to help shape this project into what it is today.

Big thanks to all of the parents, educators, medical professionals, and children who volunteered to review the books and offered such valuable feedback.

Contents

Find Your Own Glasses...

Inside The Back Cover

Preface

Know Yourself provides young learners with the building blocks they need to start their unique journey of self-discovery. Our starting point is an understanding of human anatomy—literally how we are put together. Having a general knowledge about the human body creates an empowering context on which any individual can build.

Learning about the body and mind at a young age sets the foundation for honoring one's physical form, develops self-esteem and self-confidence, and begins the discovery of who we are meant to be in this world.

Now that's real power.

Welcome!

Want to know your body's secrets?
It's amazing what's inside!
I'll help you learn about yourself.
Hello, I'm Dr. Bonyfide!

Come on a guided tour with me.
Know yourself inside and out.
We'll start with the powerful bones,
as we go along our route.

Your skeleton is a puzzle.
And these parts, they interlock.
But instead of puzzle pieces,
each bone is a building block.

Yes, these bones have names and functions,
for you to learn about.
With discoveries everywhere,
my fun rhymes will help you out.

And before you even know it,
you'll have learned them all with ease.
You'll sing and say the names of bones
just like your ABCs!

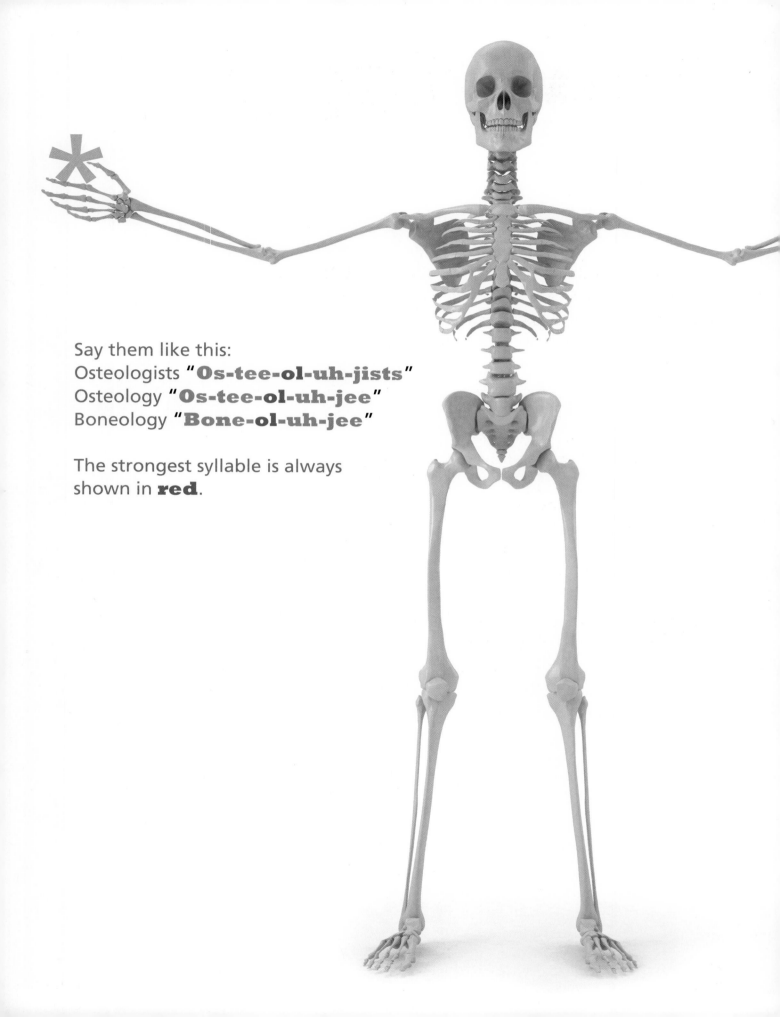

Say them like this:
Osteologists **"Os-tee-ol-uh-jists"**
Osteology **"Os-tee-ol-uh-jee"**
Boneology **"Bone-ol-uh-jee"**

The strongest syllable is always shown in **red**.

Boneology

In these books I'll teach you about all **206** bones.
Can you believe that's how many you'll own?
Some doctors are experts at all **206**.
They call themselves **osteologists**.*

Osteology* means the study of bones.
It's a word that doctors use.
To make it fun, here's a made-up word—
Boneology* is the word we choose.

"**ology**" at the end of a word
means *the study of*, you see.
And you will learn about your bones.
It's cool to learn Boneology!

Complete this book and you will find
much more knowledge in your mind.
You will earn your own degree
and be an expert in **Boneology!**

Let's start with the big picture.
Tap your knees, feel your chin.
There's something hard
underneath the skin.

What is it exactly?
You're feeling your bones—
    your living skeletal framework.
Humans are born with about 300 bones.
As we grow, some bones fuse together,
leaving us with 206 bones in the adult
    human body.

What do you think your bones do?

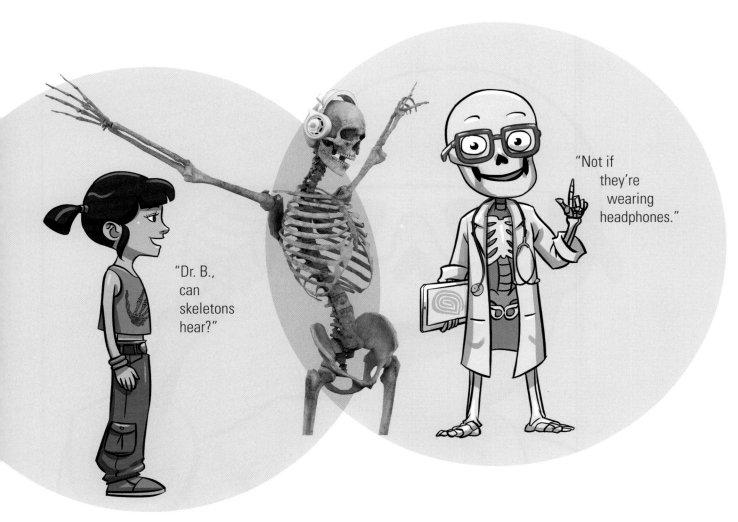

"Dr. B., can skeletons hear?"

"Not if they're wearing headphones."

Bones have four main functions:

1. **Structure**: Your skeleton forms the living framework to support and shape your body.

2. **Protection**: Your skeleton guards internal organs like the brain, heart, and lungs.

3. **Production and Storage**: Your skeleton produces red blood cells and stores minerals like calcium and phosphorous.

4. **Movement**: Your muscles attach to your skeleton, allowing your body to move.

Doctors can view the bones in your body with an X-ray machine.

Bonyfide Buddies, to start exploring, remove the X-ray glasses from the back of the book.

Upper Extremities

You can feel some of your bones,
     but you can't see them.
Feel your hand. How many bones do
     you feel?
How many bones can you feel in your arm?
How many bones do you feel in
     your shoulder?

In this book, you're going to learn
the names and locations of the
bones of the UPPER EXTREMITIES.
Say it like this: "**x-strem-i-teez**"

Upper extremities are the bones of your
hands, arms, and shoulders. There are 32
on the right side of your body and 32 on
the left side. Add them all up and write
your answer in the box below.

BONE-US MATH:

$$
\begin{array}{r}
32 \\
+\ 32 \\
\hline
\end{array}
$$

= _____ bones in the upper extremities

We will begin with your hands, starting
with the fingers.

The hand is the

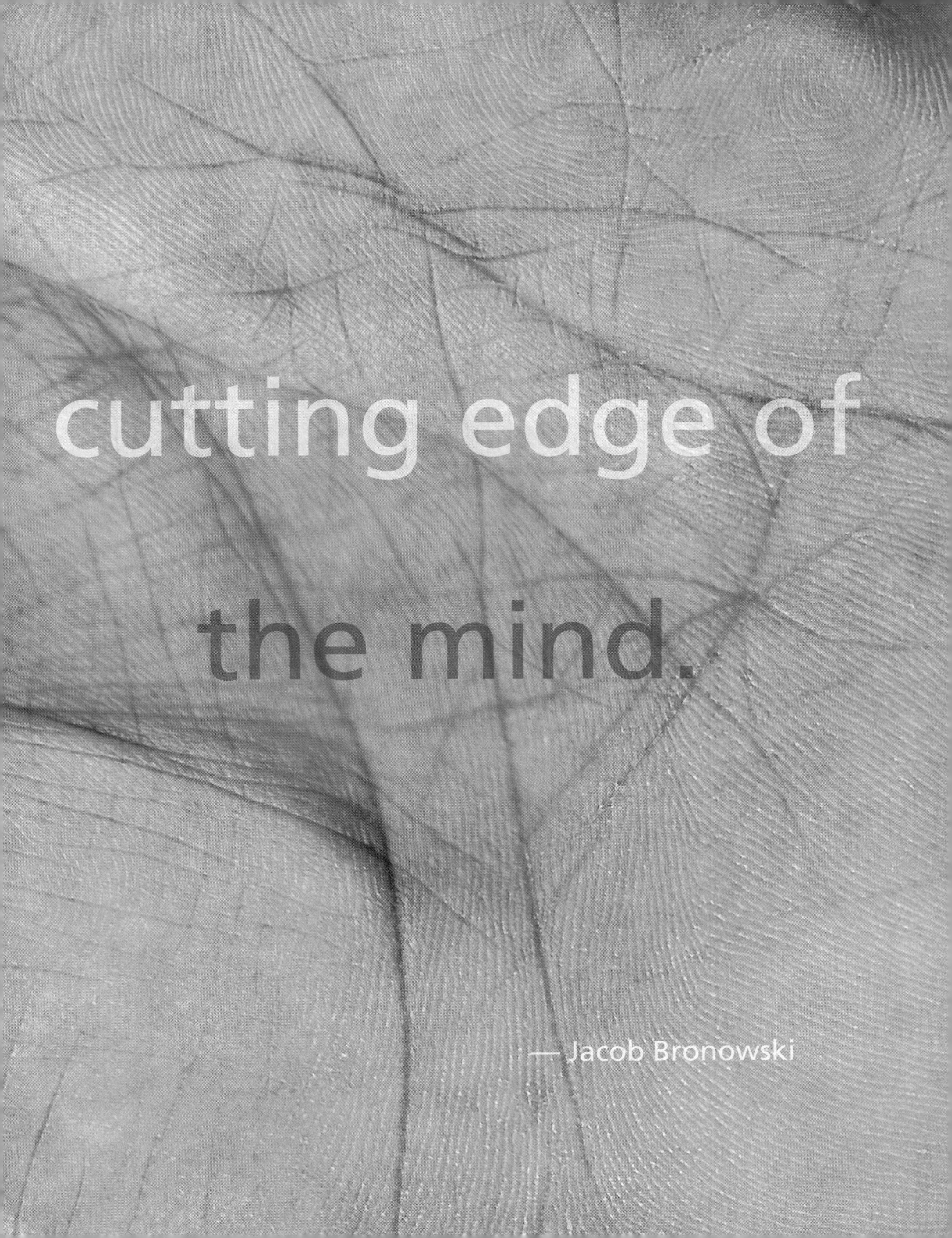

cutting edge of

the mind.

— Jacob Bronowski

Phalanges

Say it like this: **"fa-lan-geez"**

The 14 bones of your fingers are called phalanges.

What can you do with your phalanges?

What can you…

FLIP: _____

FOLD: _____

FORM: _____

Let's **DIP** into the phalanges to get a better grip.
We'll show you a word-trick, to give your brain a tip!
The word-trick is called a mnemonic.
And you say it like this: "**ne-mon-ick**"

Here's how it works:
The letters D-I-P help you remember the bones of the fingers.

D stands for the Distals. They are out at the tips.
I stands for the Intermediates. They are the bones in the middle.
P stands for the Proximals. They are the bones at the base.

Your thumb has two bones and your other fingers have three.
Take a look at your own hand and you will clearly see.

BONE-US MATH:

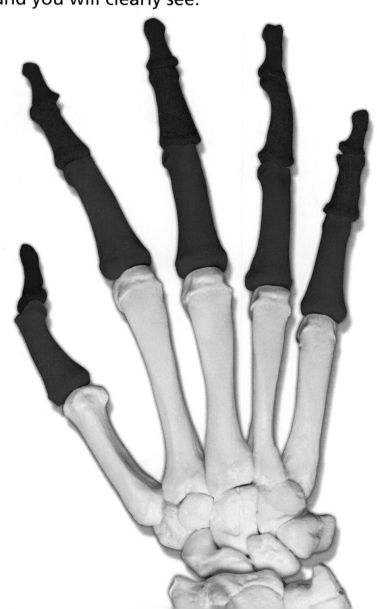

  5 Distal phalanges

+ 4 Intermediate phalanges

+ 5 Proximal phalanges
_____

=   phalanges in each hand

Distal Phalanges

Say it like this: "**dis-tull**"

The five distal phalanges are on the tips, right under your fingernails.

When used with your thumb, they help your hand grip.

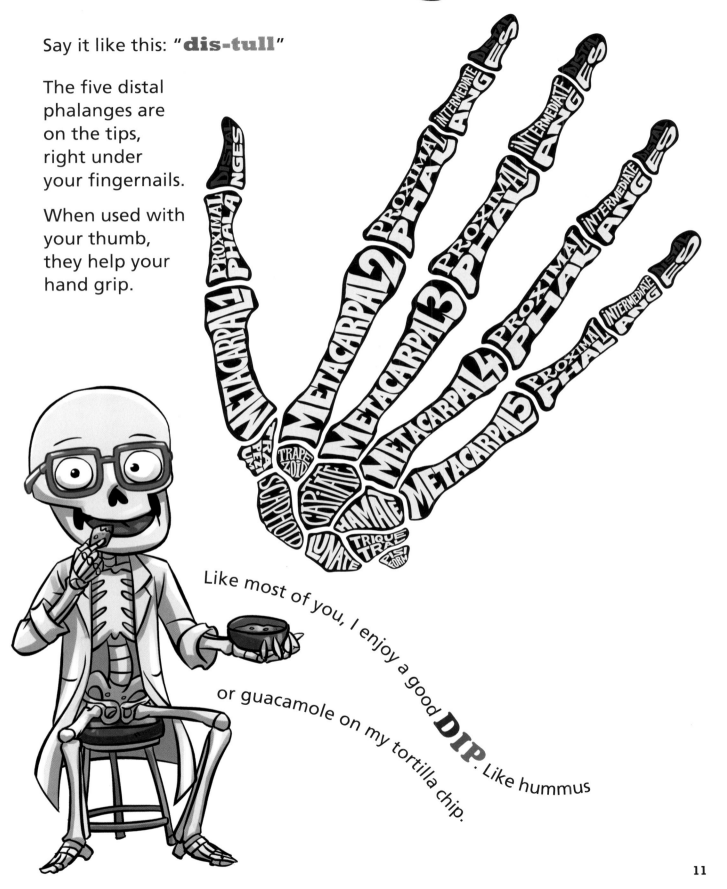

Like most of you, I enjoy a good **DIP**. Like hummus or guacamole on my tortilla chip.

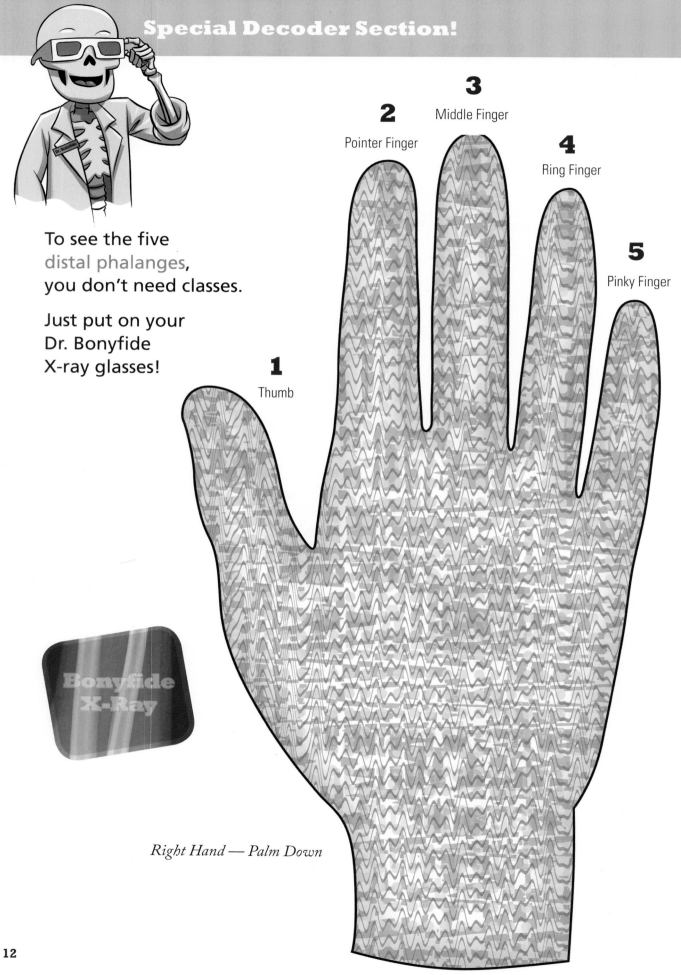

To see the five
distal phalanges,
you don't need classes.

Just put on your
Dr. Bonyfide
X-ray glasses!

2 Pointer Finger

3 Middle Finger

4 Ring Finger

5 Pinky Finger

1 Thumb

Bonyfide
X-Ray

Right Hand — Palm Down

Phalanges

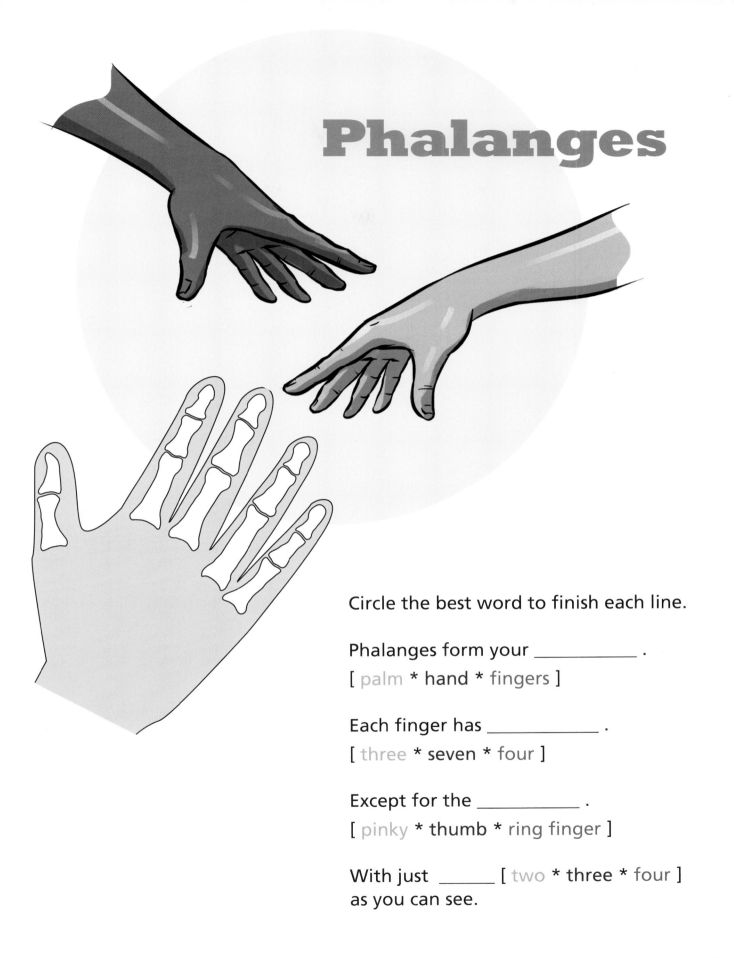

Circle the best word to finish each line.

Phalanges form your _____ .
[palm * hand * fingers]

Each finger has _____ .
[three * seven * four]

Except for the _____ .
[pinky * thumb * ring finger]

With just _____ [two * three * four]
as you can see.

Activity: Distal Phalanges

Bonyfide Buddies, it's time to draw. Trace your hand on this page.
Draw in your 5 distal phalanges at the tips. Then color them in.

Activity: Distal Phalanges

Use a distal phalange to slide through the guitar maze.

Start

Finish

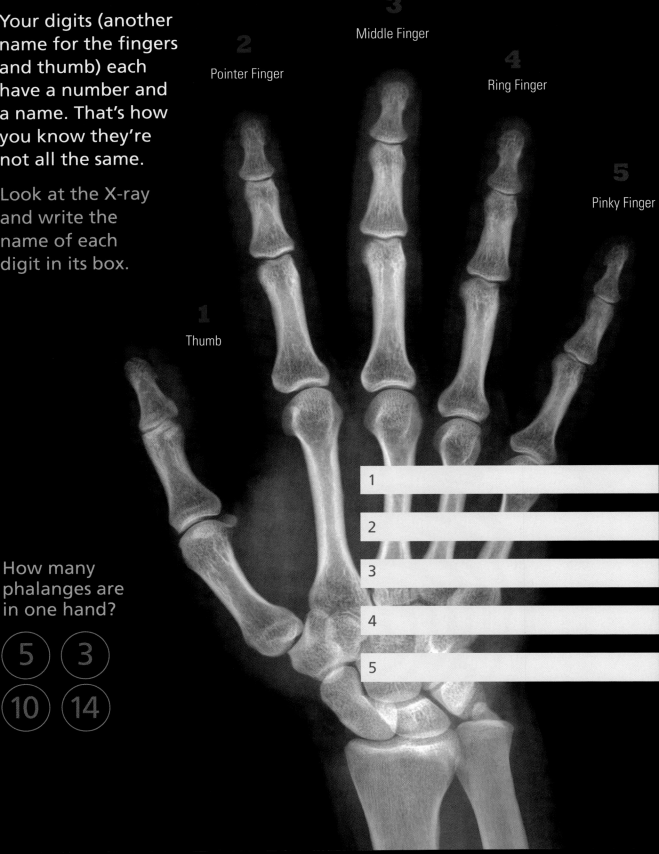

Your digits (another name for the fingers and thumb) each have a number and a name. That's how you know they're not all the same.

Look at the X-ray and write the name of each digit in its box.

How many phalanges are in one hand?

5   3

10   14

2 Pointer Finger

3 Middle Finger

4 Ring Finger

5 Pinky Finger

1 Thumb

1

2

3

4

5

Using fingerspelling, you can spell words with your **distal**, **intermediate**, and **proximal** phalanges.

Look at the way your thumb and fingers bend.

Spell "B-O-N-E" with your phalanges.

Now try it with a friend.

Can you spell "B-O-N-E" with your phalanges?

Fun Fact: *The anatomical name for thumb is pollex.*

H A N D

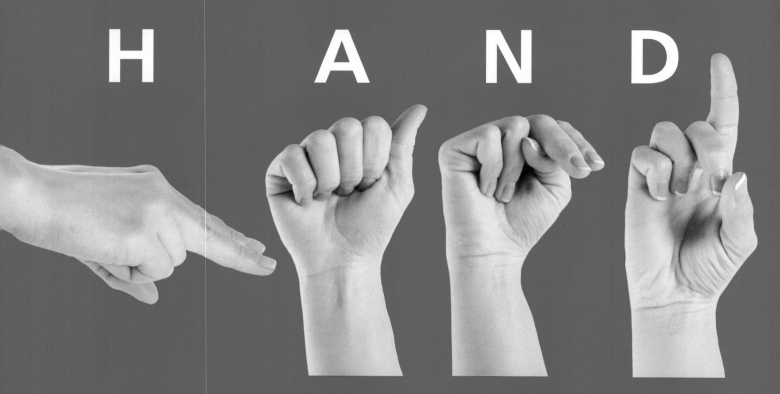

Look at the way your thumb and fingers bend.

Spell "H-A-N-D" with your phalanges.
Now try with a friend.

Can you spell "H-A-N-D" with your phalanges?

Use the Fingerspelling Alphabet to find and
spell the letters of your own name.

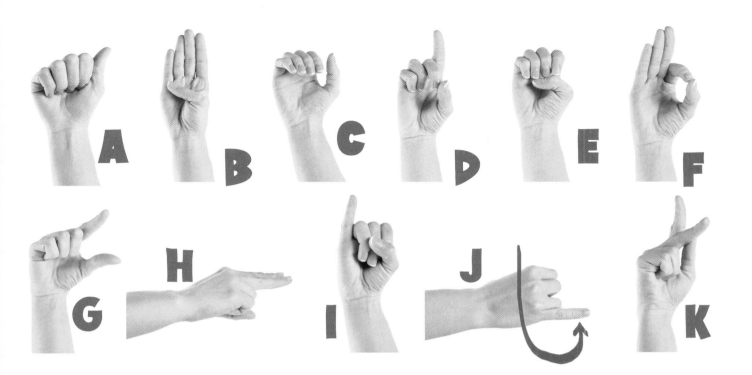

Fingerspelling Alphabet

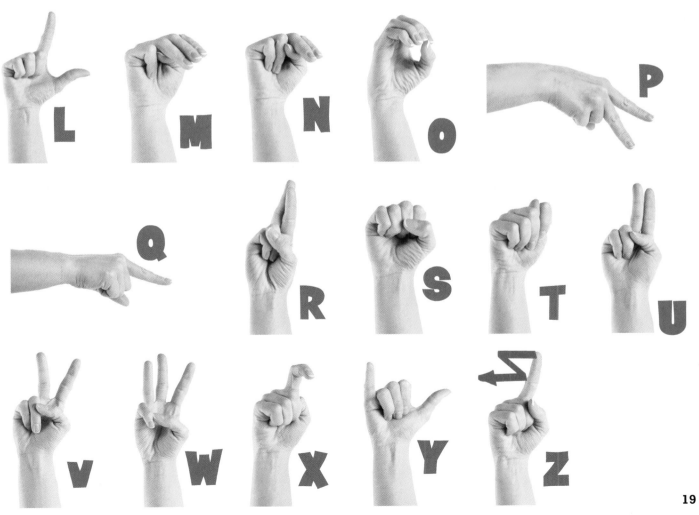

Intermediate Phalanges

Say it like this:
"in-ter-mee-dee-it"

The intermediate phalanges are the bones below the distals in the pointer, middle, ring, and pinky fingers.

Your thumb is shorter because it does not have an intermediate phalange bone.

Count the intermediates. How many intermediate phalanges are in each hand?

If you said four, you are correct.

Fun Fact: *The Statue of Liberty's pointer fingers are 8 feet long!*

Intermediate phalanges make your fingers long.
Conductors use long fingers to orchestrate a
song, or to get the Bonyfide choir to sing along!

Activity: Intermediate Phalanges

Circle the best word to finish each line.

Intermediate phalanges make your fingers

_____.

[short * pinky * long * distal]

Conductors use long

_____ to orchestrate a song,

[bones * rings * thumbs * fingers]

or to get the Bonyfide

_____

to sing along.

[music * pinky * choir * thumb]

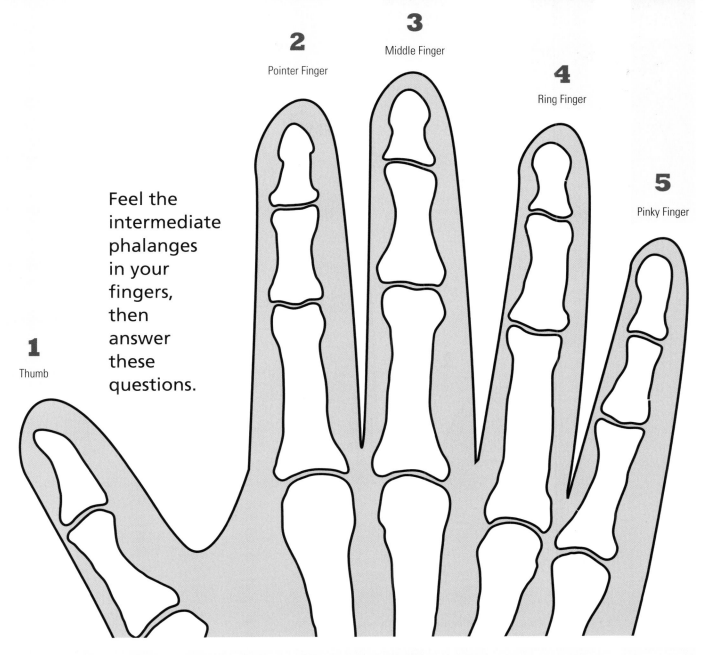

2
Pointer Finger

3
Middle Finger

4
Ring Finger

5
Pinky Finger

Feel the intermediate phalanges in your fingers, then answer these questions.

1
Thumb

1. How many intermediate phalanges are in each finger?

2. How many intermediate phalanges are in each hand?

3. Which digit does not have an intermediate phalange?

4. How many intermediate phalanges are in the thumb?

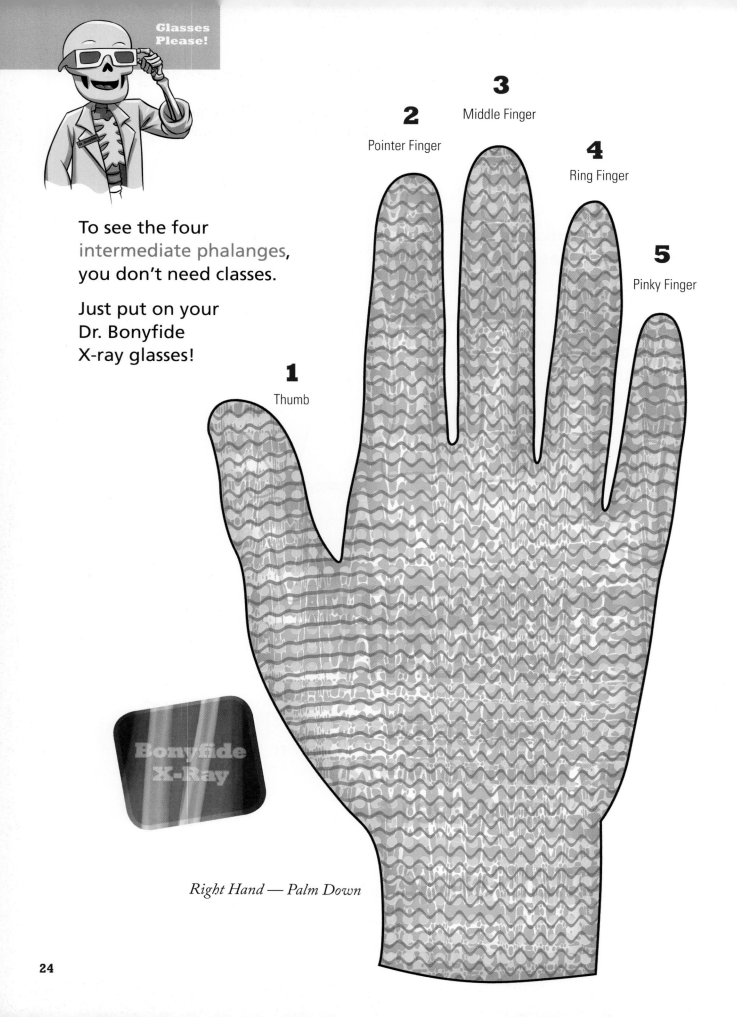

To see the four intermediate phalanges, you don't need classes.

Just put on your Dr. Bonyfide X-ray glasses!

3 Middle Finger

2 Pointer Finger

4 Ring Finger

5 Pinky Finger

1 Thumb

Bonyfide X-Ray

Right Hand — Palm Down

Activity: Intermediate Phalanges

Time to draw! Trace your hand on this page. Draw in the 5 distal and 4 intermediate phalanges. Now color them in. There should be 9 phalanges when you are done.

Proximal Phalanges

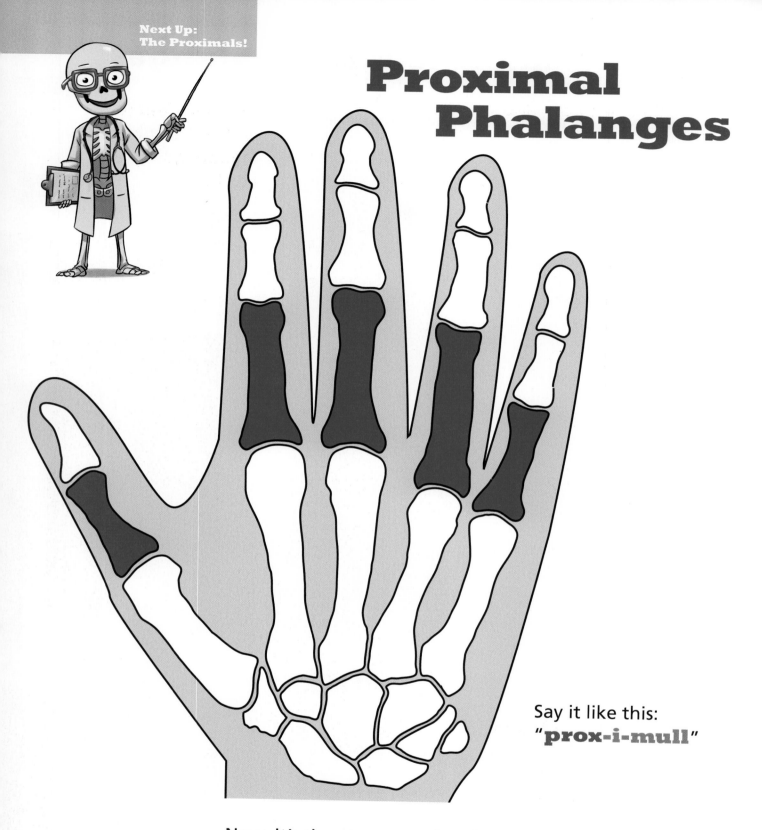

Say it like this:
"prox-i-mull"

Now, it's time to move ahead to the final set of phalanges, the proximals. They sit at the base of your fingers.

The word "proximal" means nearest something.
The proximal phalanges are the bones nearest your palm.

Can you find your proximal phalanges?

26

Bones can break.
With time, they can also
heal themselves.

Doctors often use
casts to keep bones
immobile so they
can heal.

Look at these X-rays.
What do you see?

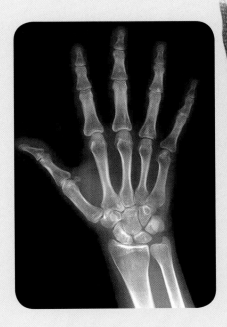

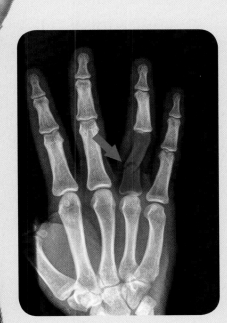

The one on the left shows
a normal ring finger. The
one on the right shows
a broken ring finger.

Which phalange bone is broken?

_____

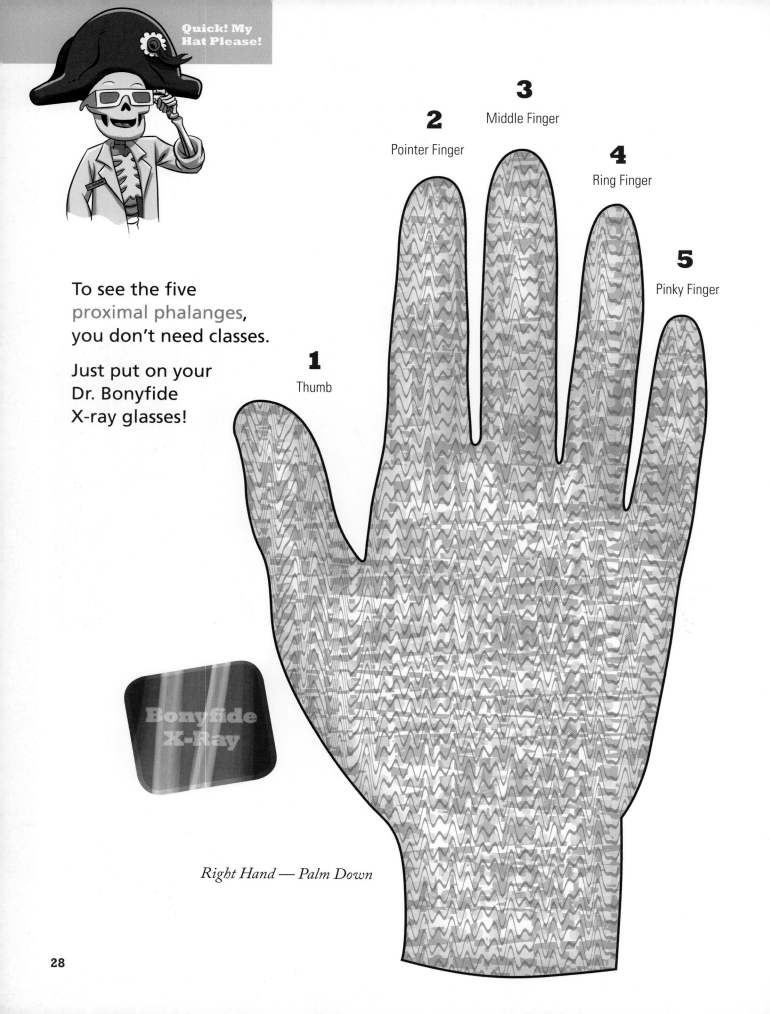

3 Middle Finger

2 Pointer Finger

4 Ring Finger

5 Pinky Finger

To see the five proximal phalanges, you don't need classes.

Just put on your Dr. Bonyfide X-ray glasses!

1 Thumb

Bonyfide X-Ray

Right Hand — Palm Down

Activity: Phalanges

First, trace your hand. Starting at the tips, draw in the 5 distal phalanges. Next, draw in the 4 intermediate phalanges, followed by the 5 proximal phalanges. Did you draw in all 14 bones? Now color them in.

Phalanges Review

Fill in the blanks:

1. There are five

_____

phalanges close to your palm.

2. There are four

_____

phalanges in the middle of your fingers.

3. There are five

_____ phalanges at the tips of your fingers.

4. How many phalanges are in one hand?

_____

BONE-US MATH:

_____ Distals

+ _____ Intermediates

+ _____ Proximals

= _____ phalanges

Name the **three** parts of your phalanges:

D _____ at the tips.

I _____ in the middle.

P _____ at the base.

Metacarpals

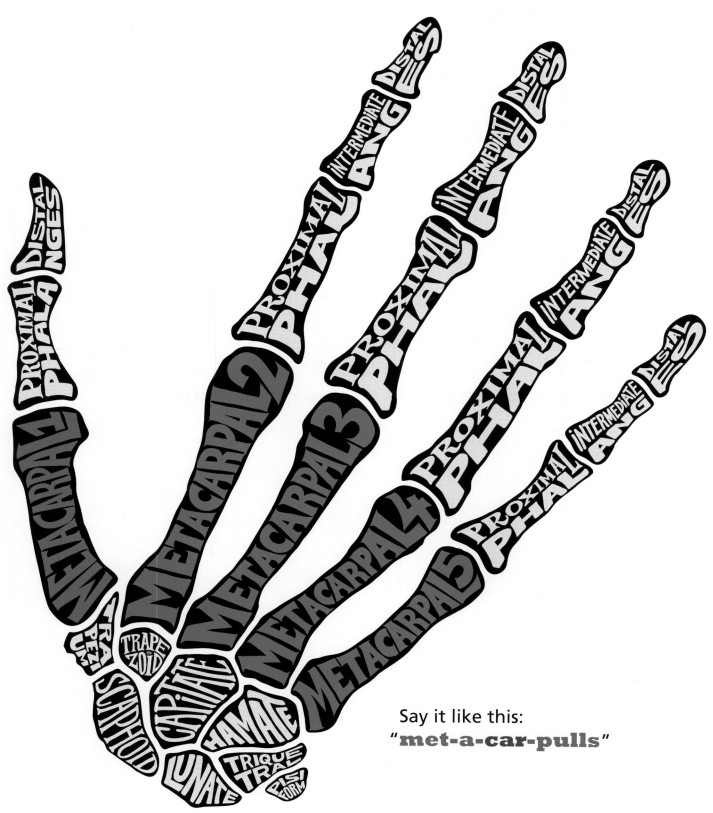

Say it like this:
"met-a-car-pulls"

Your palm is made of five metacarpal bones.

The metacarpal names are simply numbers:

1
2
3
4
5

Metacarpal # **1** extends your thumb.

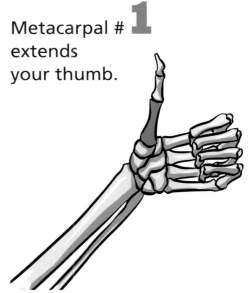

Metacarpal # **2** points your index finger for you.

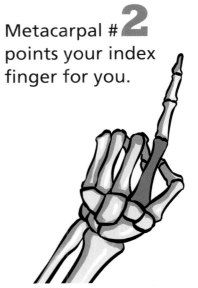

Metacarpal # **3** makes a peace sign easily.

The Metacarpal 5!

Metacarpal #**4** sits under that ring that you adore.

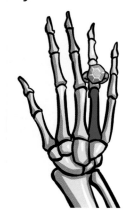

Metacarpal #**5** helps your pinky come alive!

Bonyfide Buddies, clap your **metacarpals** together and give the band a big round of applause!

The metacarpal names are simply 1, 2, 3, 4, 5.
Use them to bust out the Bonyfide Hand Jive.

It's a dance with your hands that moves rapid-fire.
It's eight counts in all. Come on! Get inspired!

Slap **1**

Slap **2**

Clap **3**

Clap **4**

Criss **5**

Cross **6**

Snap **7**

Snap **8**

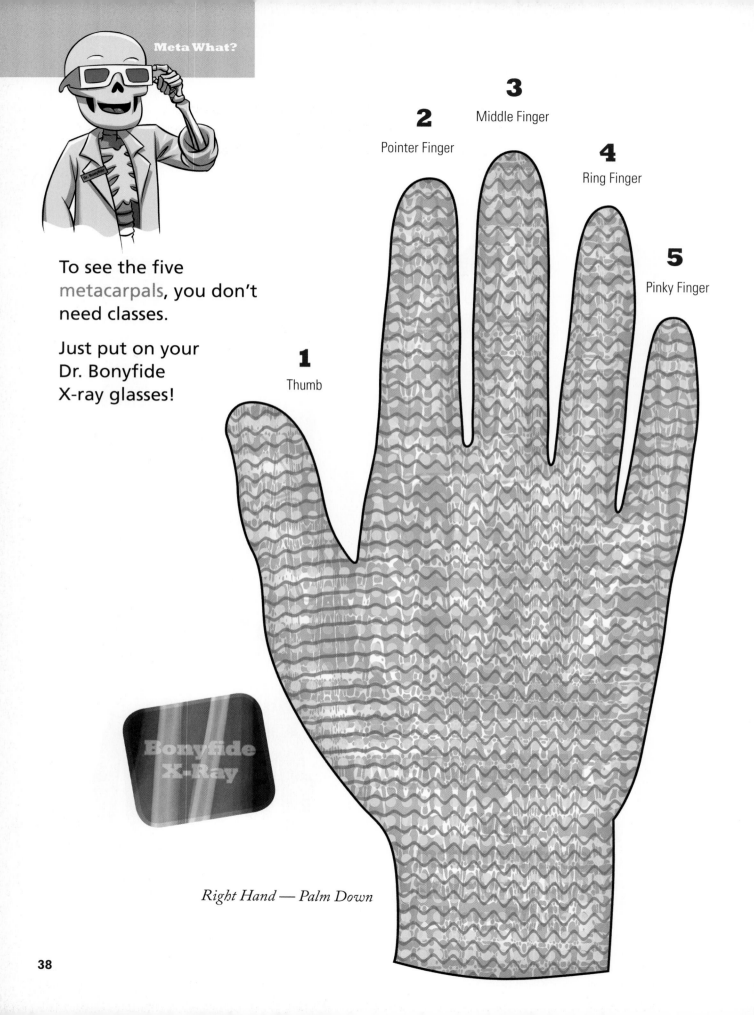

To see the five metacarpals, you don't need classes.

Just put on your Dr. Bonyfide X-ray glasses!

2 Pointer Finger

3 Middle Finger

4 Ring Finger

5 Pinky Finger

1 Thumb

Right Hand — Palm Down

Activity: Metacarpals

First, trace your hand on this page. Then draw in the bones of your hand: 5 distals, 4 intermediates, 5 proximals, and 5 metacarpals. That's a lot of bones! How many bones have you drawn? ____. Starting with the thumb, number the metacarpals 1, 2, 3, 4, 5. Finish by coloring them all in.

ALL ABOARD, BONYFIDE BUDDIES!

If you're ready for more,
then head for the door.
Our first stop is Carpal Junction
where we'll find out how our wrist
bones function.

Meeting us there is Pinky Le Darpals,
the resident expert on what else—
the carpals!

When you count them all up
they number eight.
With Pinky on board,
she'll set you straight.

Carpals

Say it like this: **"car-pulls"**

WOW! *COOL!*

The carpals sit in two rows between your palm and your wrist. Their unique shapes help your wrist bend and twist.

Let's take the train to Proximal Plaza where we'll look more closely at the proximal carpals.

Proximal Carpals

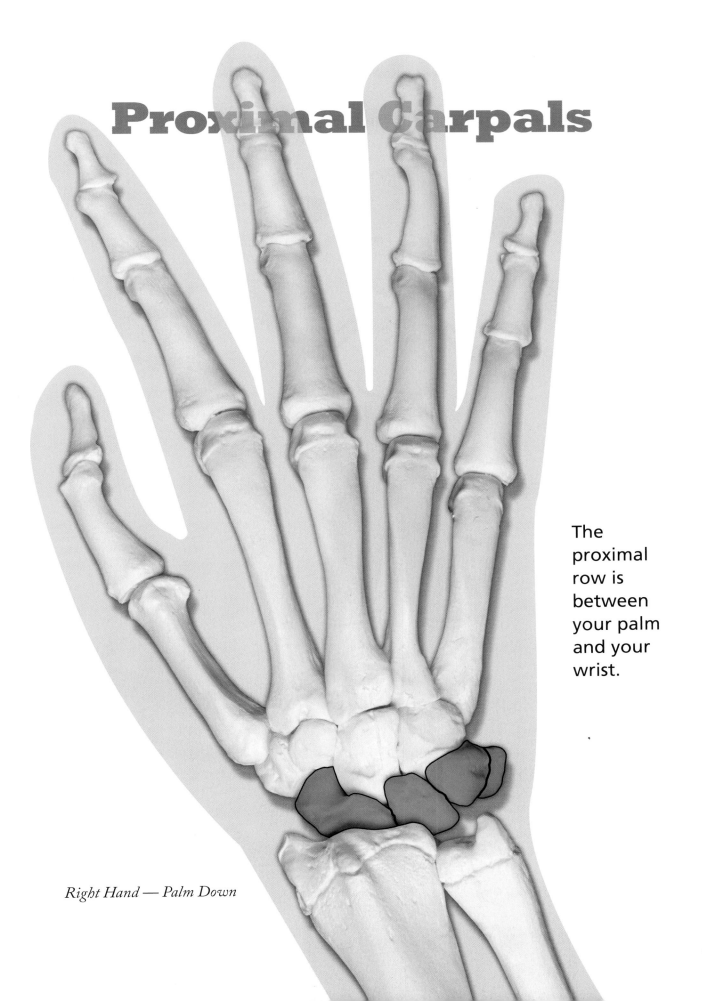

The proximal row is between your palm and your wrist.

Right Hand — Palm Down

Proximal Carpals

Presenting the proximal carpals. Give them a glance.
We'll learn each one in a fun circumstance!

The four proximal
carpals:

"Say it like this:"

Scaphoid   "**skaf-oid**"
Lunate   "**loo-nate**"
Triquetral   "**try-kwee-troll**"
Pisiform   "**pie-sa-form**"

The word "proximal" means
nearest something. The
proximal carpals are nearest
to, and connect to your
forearm bones.

We do so many things with our carpals: writing our names, brushing our teeth, bouncing a ball, and playing the drums.

Rotate your wrists. Move them side to side. Write a few things your wrists help you do:

_____   _____

_____   _____

"So Long To Pinky"

"So Long To Pinky" is my mnemonic word-trick to help you remember the names of the proximal carpals. Write the name of the bone down from the first letter of each word.

It'll look like this:

So	**Long**	**To**	**Pinky**
C	U	R	I
A	N	I	S
P	A	Q	I
H	T	U	F
O	E	E	O
I		T	R
D		R	M
		A	
		L	

Now you try it:

So Long To Pinky

_____ _____   _____ _____

_____ _____   _____ _____

_____ _____   _____

_____ _____   _____

_____ _____   _____

_____ _____   _____

_____   _____

                             _____

*A mnemonic helps your memory. The "m" is silent. Say it like this: "ne-**mon**-ick"*

Rewrite the names of the proximal carpals here.

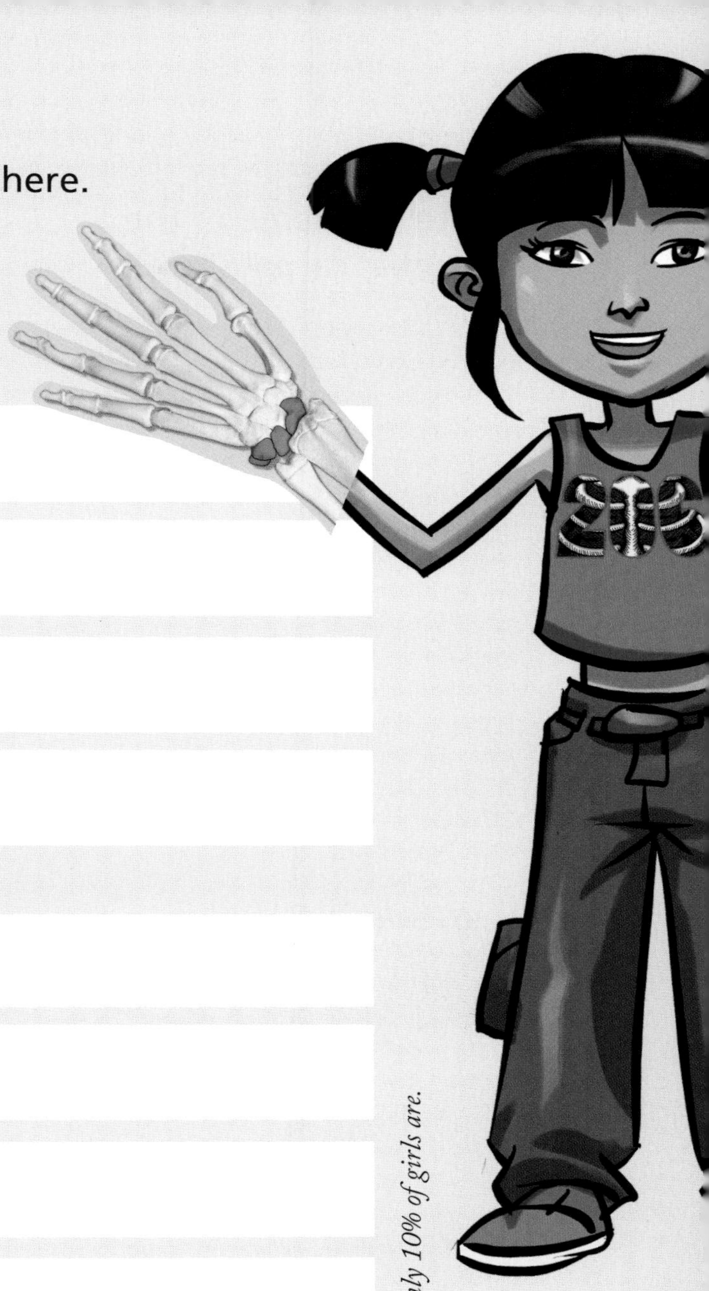

Scaphoid

Lunate

Triquetral

Pisiform

Triquetral

Lunate

Pisiform

Scaphoid

Pisiform

Scaphoid

Lunate

Triquetral

Fun Fact: *12% of all boys are left-handed, while only 10% of girls are.*

Write the name of the proximal carpal shown in red.

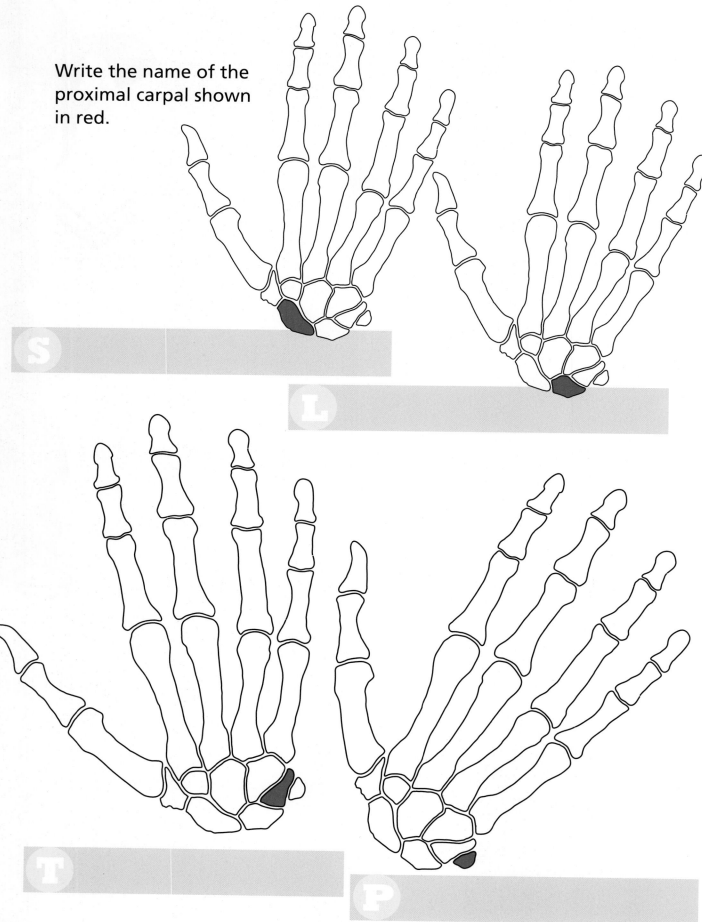

S

L

T

P

"What does this Latin sign say below? "

Etymology

Say it like this:
"et-a-mol-a-jee"

Etymology means
the root of the word,
or how it began.

Some are quite funny,
some are quite bland.

Carpal names come from
Latin or Greek.

They describe familiar
things. Let's take a peek.

NOSCE
TE
IPSUM

CARPALS: Scaphoid

The first carpal we'll learn is the scaphoid.

Say it like this: "**skaf-oid**"

Scaphoid comes from the Greek word *skaphos*, meaning "hollow shell" or "a kind of boat." This is what the scaphoid bone looks like.

Can you see the boat shape in the scaphoid bone?

Activity: Carpals

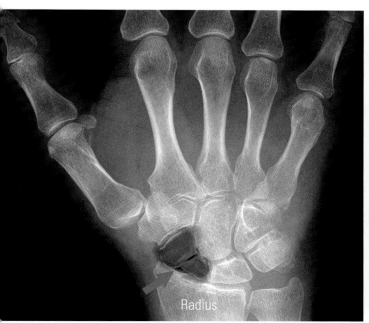

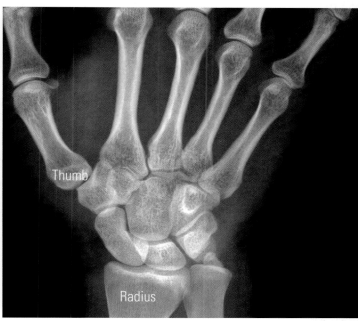

Look at the broken carpal in the X-ray.
Can you write the name of the broken carpal bone?

_____

CARPALS: Lunate

The next carpal is the lunate.

Say lunate like this: **"loo-nate"**

Lunate comes from *luna*, meaning "moon" in Latin.

The lunate bone is shaped like a crescent moon.

A crescent moon appears only partially lit. Do you see the shape of the crescent moon in the lunate carpal?

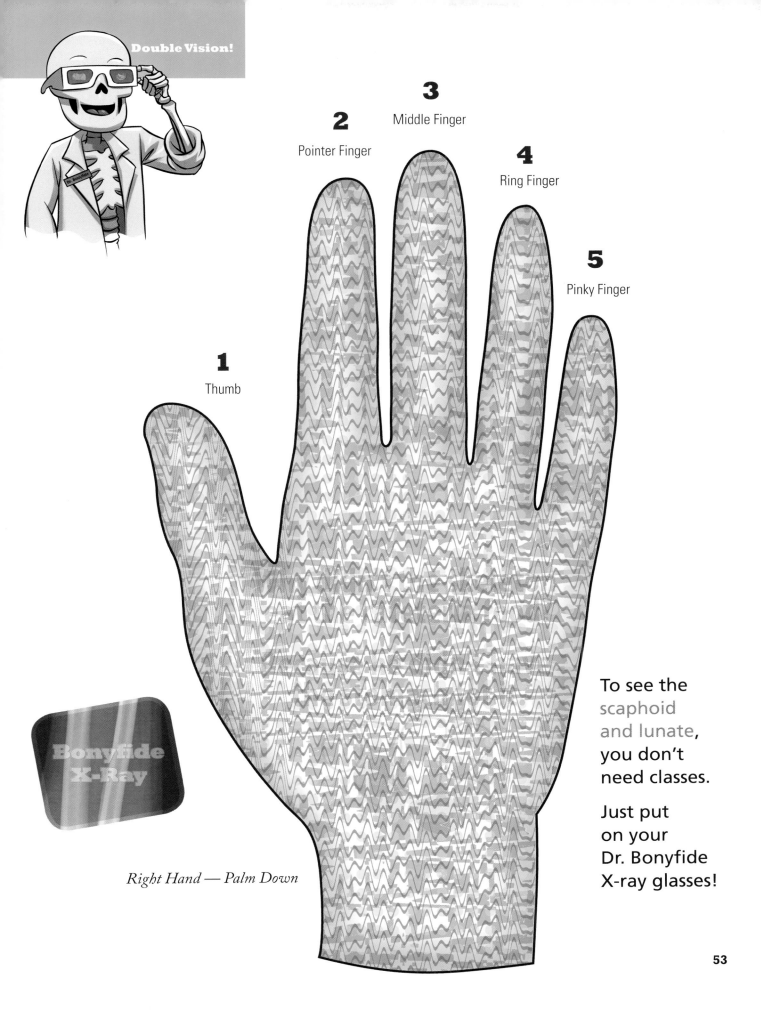

Double Vision!

2 Pointer Finger

3 Middle Finger

4 Ring Finger

5 Pinky Finger

1 Thumb

Bonyfide X-Ray

Right Hand — Palm Down

To see the scaphoid and lunate, you don't need classes.

Just put on your Dr. Bonyfide X-ray glasses!

Activity:
Scaphoid and Lunate

Say "scaphoid" and "lunate" 3 times each.
Then write them on the *line*

Scaphoid

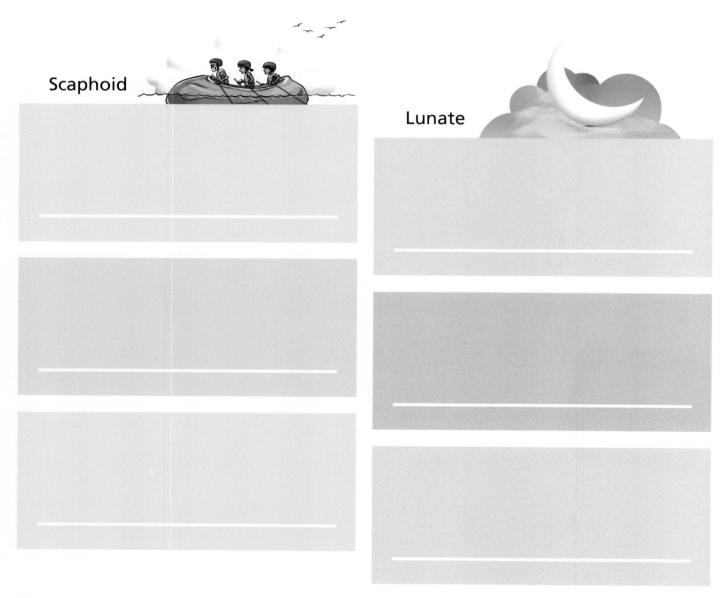

Lunate

CARPALS: Triquetral

"*These are my three cute trolls. Get it?*"

TRY **KWEE** **TROLL**

The next carpal bone is the triquetral.

Say it like this: "**try-kwee-troll**"

The name of the triquetral bone comes from the Latin word *triquetrus*, meaning "three-cornered," like a triangle.

CARPALS: Pisiform

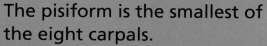

The pisiform is the smallest of the eight carpals.

Say it like this: **"pie-sa-form"**

The word pisiform comes from the Latin word *pisum*, meaning "pea." This is exactly what the small round bone resembles in size and shape. Dr. Bonyfide would rather eat pie than peas.

How about you?

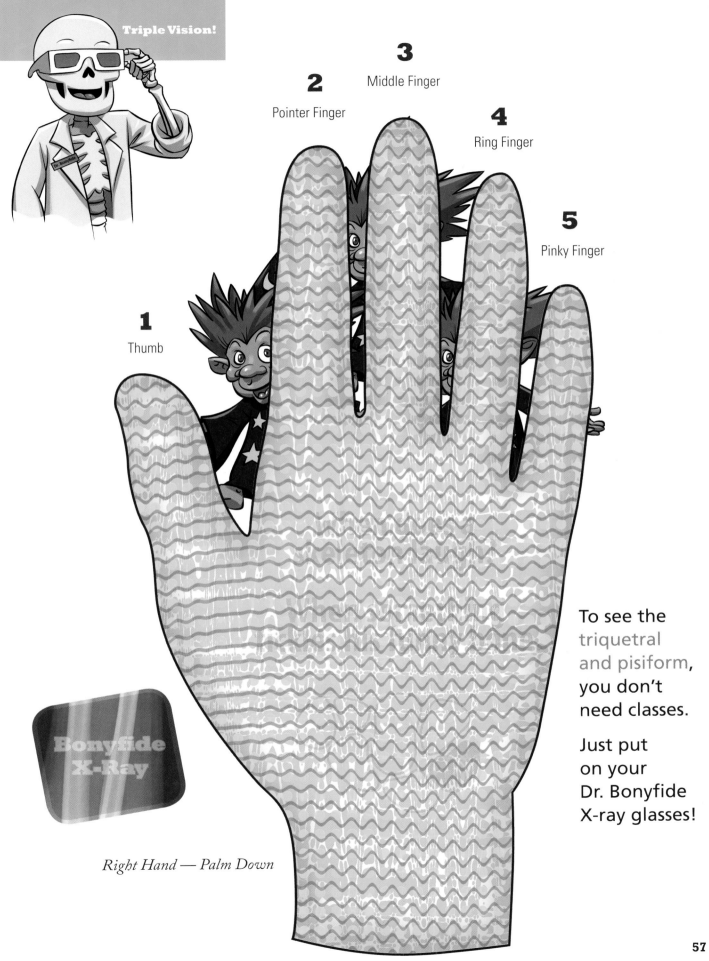

Triple Vision!

2 Pointer Finger

3 Middle Finger

4 Ring Finger

5 Pinky Finger

1 Thumb

Bonyfide X-Ray

Right Hand — Palm Down

To see the triquetral and pisiform, you don't need classes.

Just put on your Dr. Bonyfide X-ray glasses!

Activity:
Triquetral and Pisiform

Say "triquetral" and "pisiform" 3 times each. Then write them on the

line

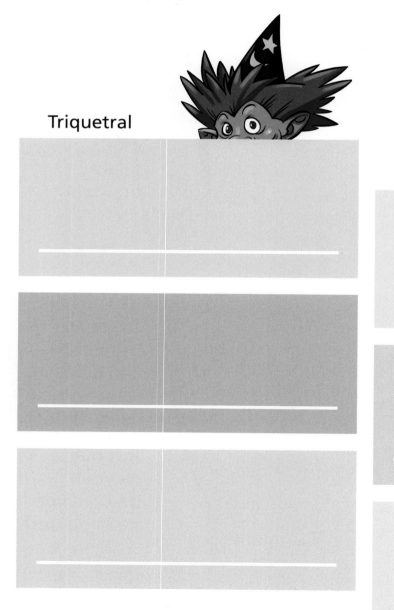

Triquetral

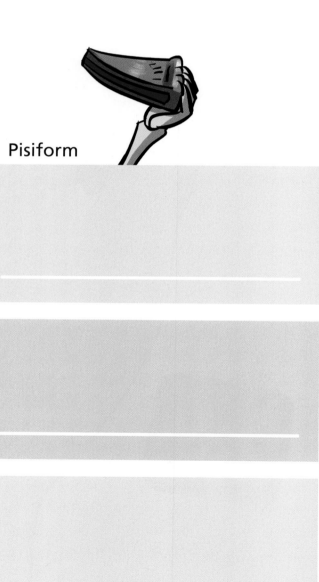

Pisiform

Activity: **Proximal Carpals**

Check the name of the highlighted bone.

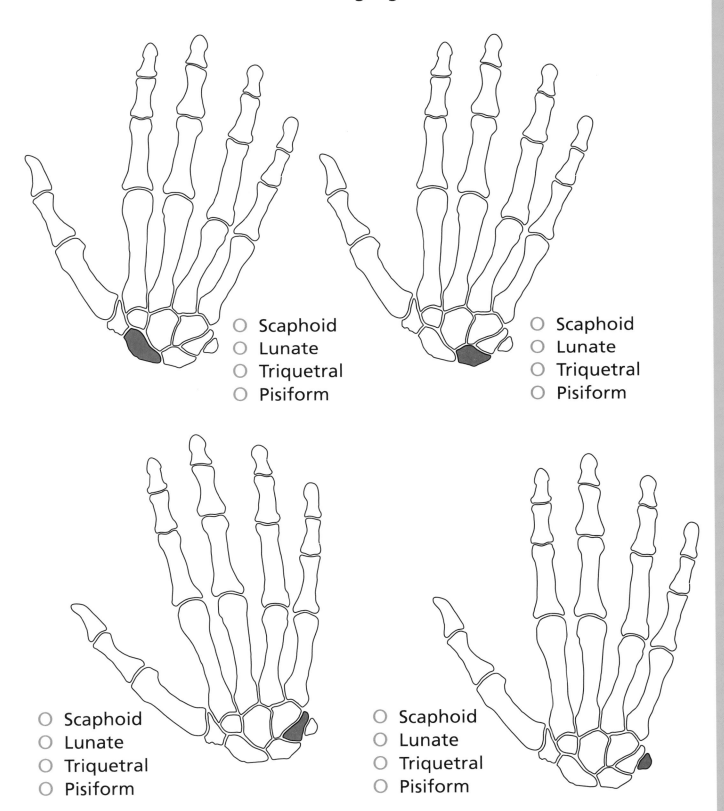

○ Scaphoid
○ Lunate
○ Triquetral
○ Pisiform

○ Scaphoid
○ Lunate
○ Triquetral
○ Pisiform

○ Scaphoid
○ Lunate
○ Triquetral
○ Pisiform

○ Scaphoid
○ Lunate
○ Triquetral
○ Pisiform

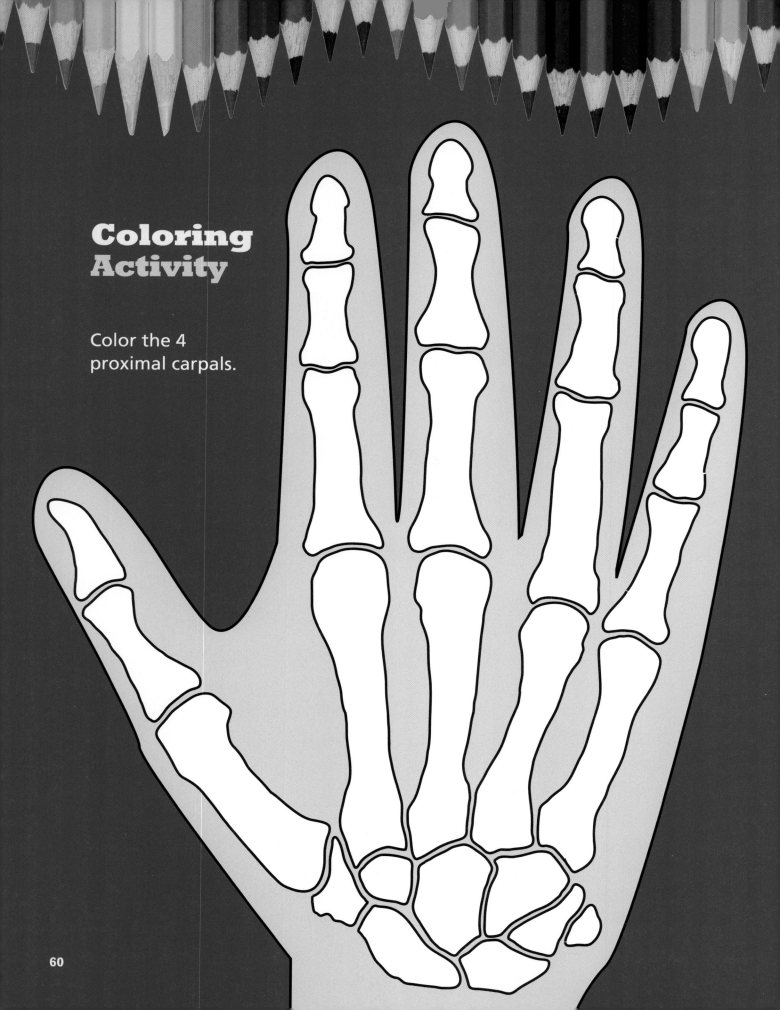

Coloring Activity

Color the 4 proximal carpals.

Distal Carpals

Good job Bonyfide Buddies! Now, let's hop on the train to Distal District, where we'll meet up with the four carpal bones in the distal row.

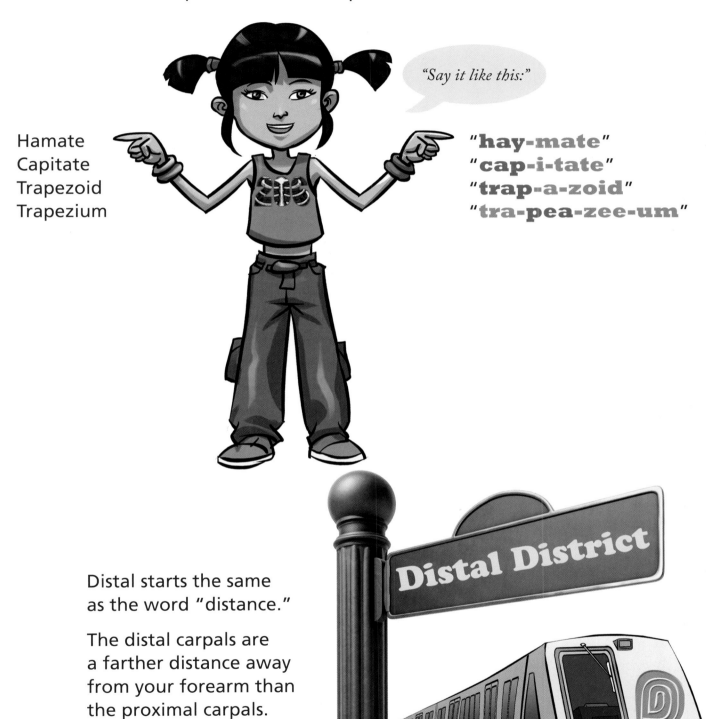

"Say it like this:"

Hamate
Capitate
Trapezoid
Trapezium

"**hay-mate**"
"**cap-i-tate**"
"**trap-a-zoid**"
"**tra-pea-zee-um**"

Distal starts the same as the word "distance."

The distal carpals are a farther distance away from your forearm than the proximal carpals.

Distal District

Distal Carpals

The distal row sits below the metacarpals of your palm.

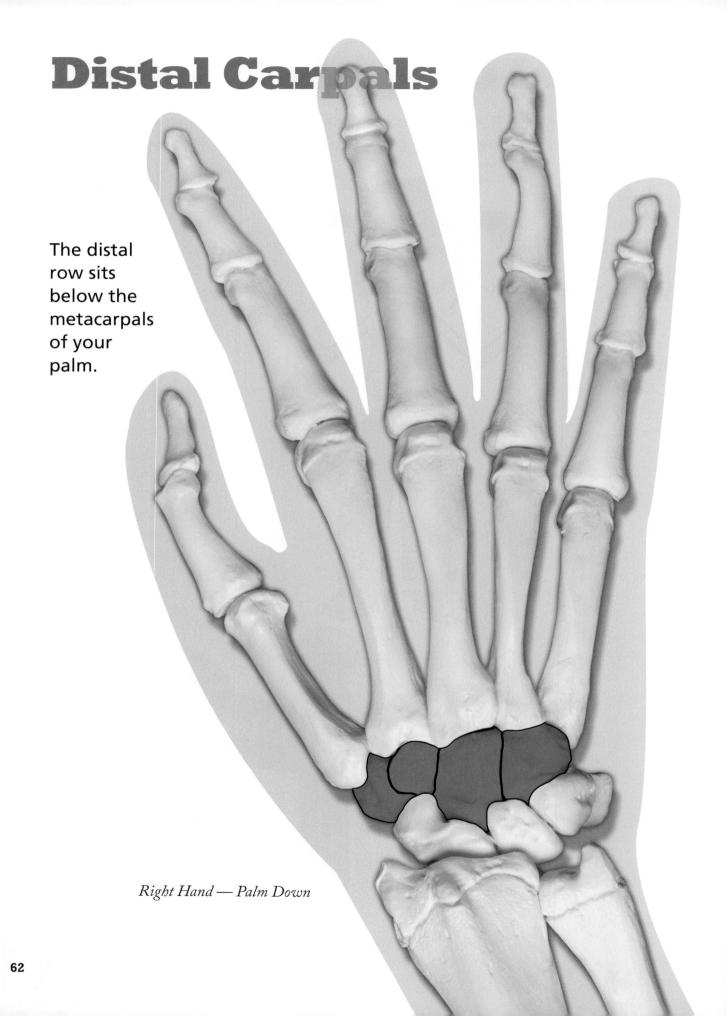

Right Hand — Palm Down

Let's use the mnemonic word-trick as before!
Write the name of the bone down from each letter.

It'll look like this:

Here	**C**omes	**T**he	**T**rain
A	A	R	R
M	P	A	A
A	I	P	P
T	T	E	E
E	A	Z	Z
	T	O	I
	E	I	U
		D	M

Now you try it:

Here Comes The Train

_____	_____	_____	_____
_____	_____	_____	_____
_____	_____	_____	_____
_____	_____	_____	_____
_____	_____	_____	_____
	_____	_____	_____
	_____	_____	_____

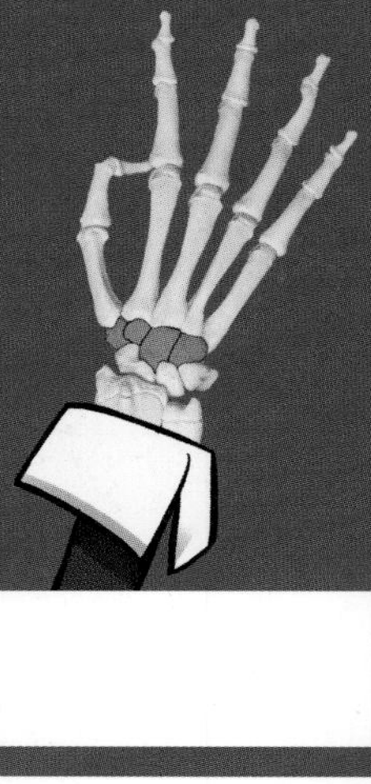

Practice writing the names of the distal carpals:

Hamate

Capitate

Trapezoid

Trapezium

Hamate

Capitate

Trapezoid

Trapezium

Hamate

Capitate

Trapezoid

Trapezium

Fun Fact: The capitate is the largest carpal bone in your wrist. It's about the size of a cashew nut.

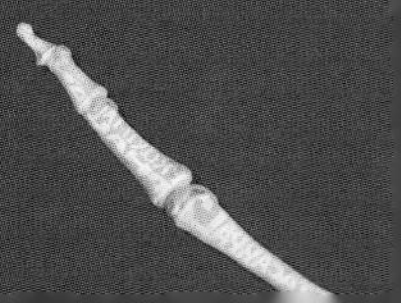

CARPALS: Hamate

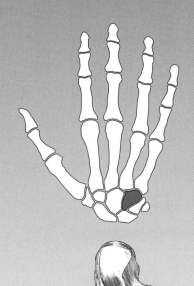

"hay-mate"

The first distal carpal we'll learn is the hamate.

Say it like this:

Hamate comes from the Latin word *hamus*, meaning "hook." One of its six surfaces looks like a little hook, so that's where hamate gets its name.

Do you see the little hook shape in this bone?

CARPALS: Capitate

The next carpal bone is the capitate.

Say it like this: **"cap-i-tate"**

Capitate comes from the Latin word *capitātus*, which means "head." Look at the picture. Do you see the smooth, rounded head of the capitate bone?

Bonyfide Buddies, did you notice that hamate and capitate rhyme? They both end in the sound "ate."

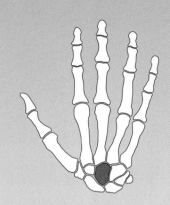

"Hey Mate! Keep your head on straight."

Squawk!

Squawk!

Fun Fact: *The capitate is the largest carpal bone in the human hand.*

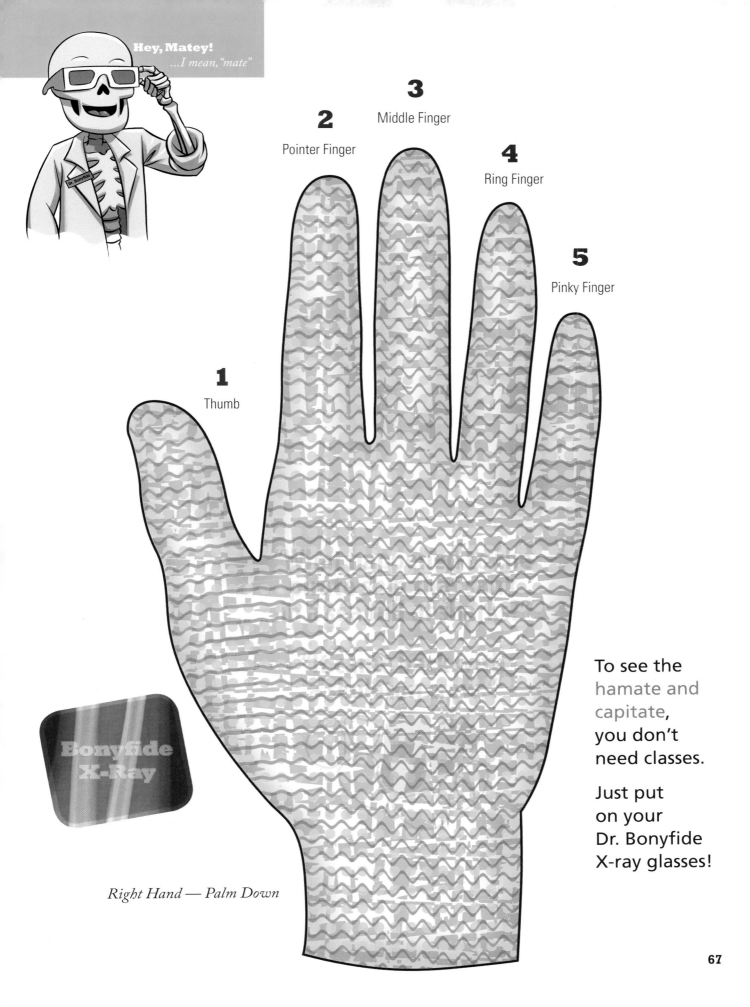

Hey, Matey!
...I mean, "mate"

3 Middle Finger

2 Pointer Finger

4 Ring Finger

5 Pinky Finger

1 Thumb

Bonyfide X-Ray

Right Hand — Palm Down

To see the hamate and capitate, you don't need classes.

Just put on your Dr. Bonyfide X-ray glasses!

Activity: Hamate and Capitate

Say "hamate" and "capitate" 3 times each
and write them in the boxes below.

Hamate

Capitate

These four carpal names might really seem tough.
You may be thinking, enough is enough!
But hold tight for a minute, be Bonyfide strong.
We're sailing right through, it won't be too long!

The next two carpals are the trapezoid and the trapezium.

Say them like this:
"trap-a-zoid" and
"tra-pea-zee-um"

Both of these words are from the Greek word *trapezion*, meaning "little table."

Did you notice that they both begin with the letters "T - R - A - P ?" Here's a little rap to remember which bone is which:

> *You cannot avoid your trapezoid*
> *when you're trying to make a point.*
> *Cause it's the thing*
> *that puts the spring*
> *in your index finger's joint!*
>
> *Underneath your thumb*
> *sits your trapezium.*
> *It has a very important function.*
> *It can touch the tips*
> *of the other digits,*
> *making it an amazing junction!*

69

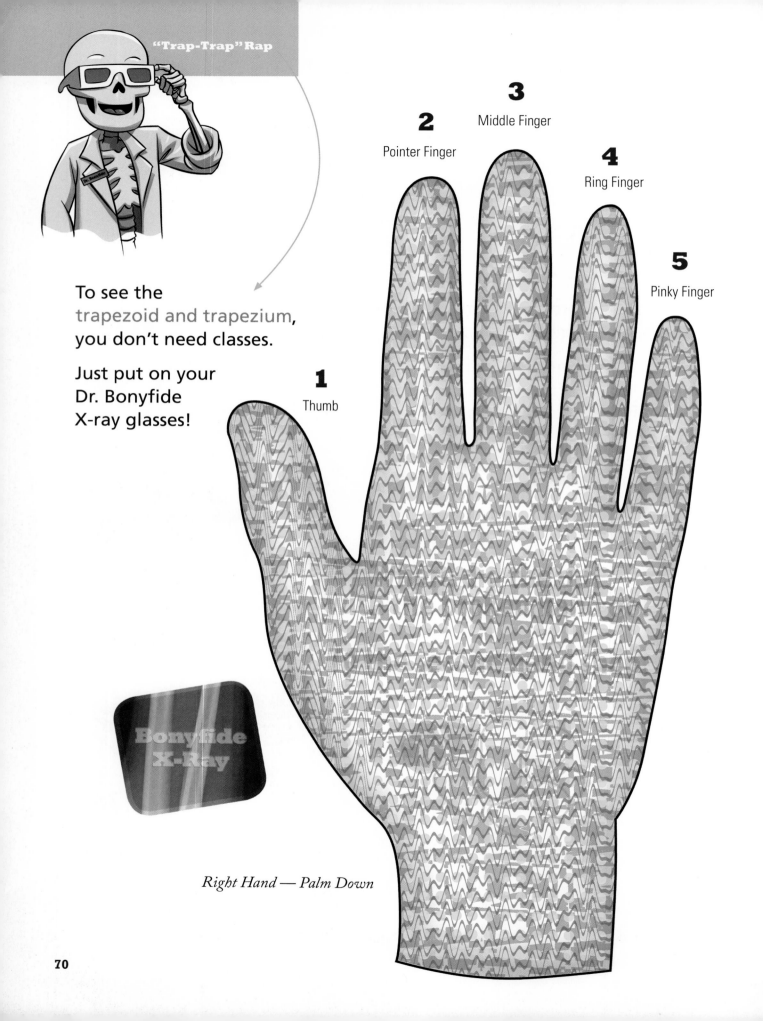

To see the
trapezoid and trapezium,
you don't need classes.

Just put on your
Dr. Bonyfide
X-ray glasses!

1 Thumb

2 Pointer Finger

3 Middle Finger

4 Ring Finger

5 Pinky Finger

Bonyfide
X-Ray

Right Hand — Palm Down

Activity: Trapezoid and Trapezium

Say "trapezoid" and "trapezium" 3 times each, then write them on the lines.

Trapezoid   Trapezium

_____   _____

_____   _____

_____   _____

Bonyfide Buddies, just remember the trapezium is under your thumb!

Activity: Distal Carpals

Check the name of the highlighted bone.

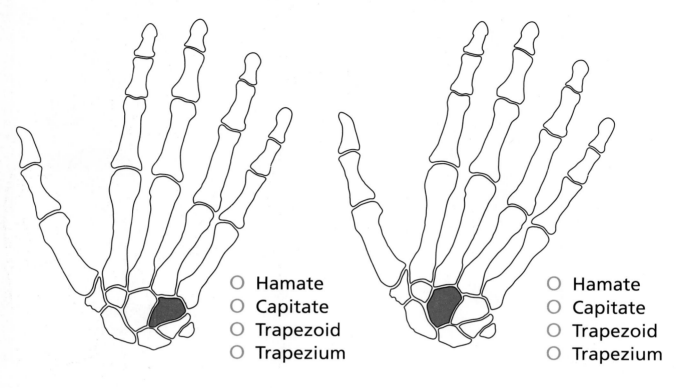

○ Hamate
○ Capitate
○ Trapezoid
○ Trapezium

○ Hamate
○ Capitate
○ Trapezoid
○ Trapezium

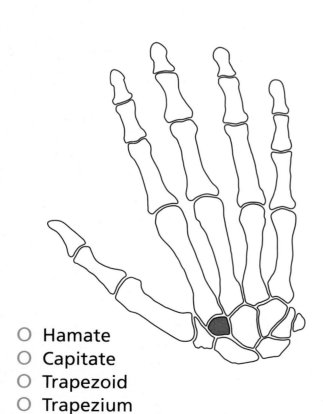

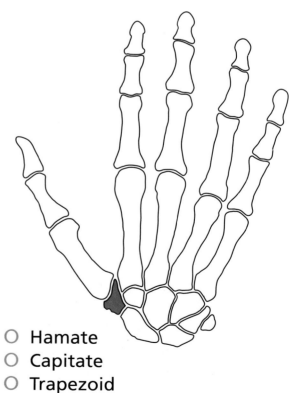

○ Hamate
○ Capitate
○ Trapezoid
○ Trapezium

○ Hamate
○ Capitate
○ Trapezoid
○ Trapezium

Activity: Distal Carpals

Color in the 4 distal carpals.

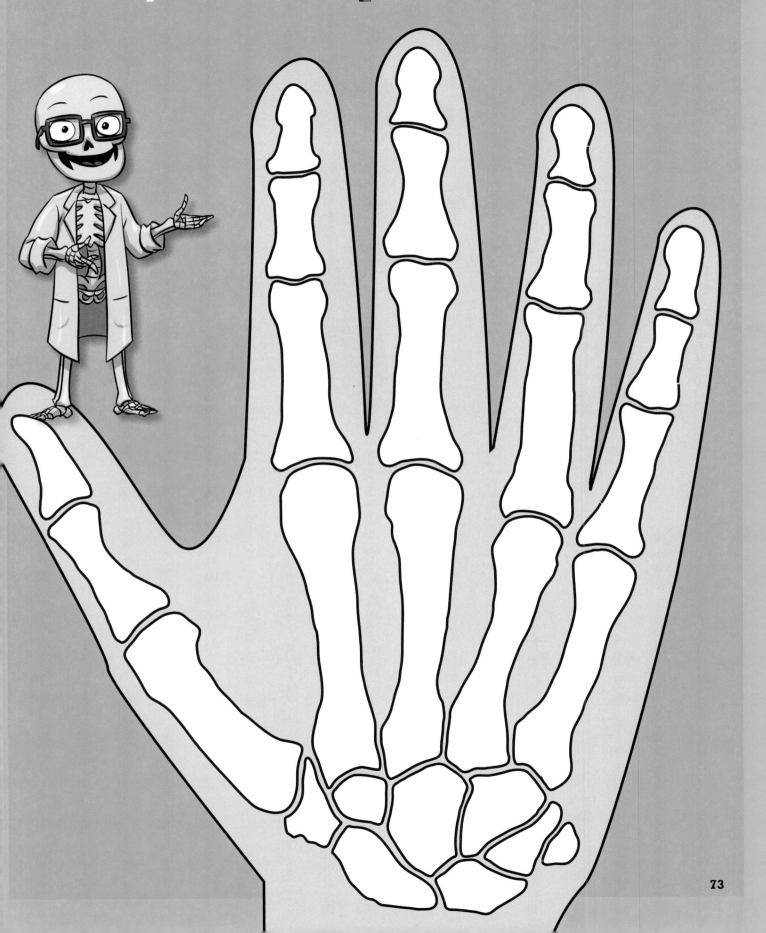

73

Activity: Carpals

Let's use our mnemonic word-trick to write all 8 carpals.

So Long To Pinky

‒‒‒‒ ‒‒‒‒

‒‒‒‒ ‒‒‒‒

‒‒‒‒ ‒‒‒‒

‒‒‒‒ ‒‒‒‒

‒‒‒‒ ‒‒‒‒

‒‒‒‒ ‒‒‒‒

‒‒‒‒

‒‒‒‒

Here Comes

‒‒‒‒

‒‒‒‒

‒‒‒‒

‒‒‒‒

‒‒‒‒

‒‒‒‒

Say it out loud, 'til it's stuck in your brain...
So Long To Pinky, Here Comes The Train!

Practice writing the names of the eight carpal bones:

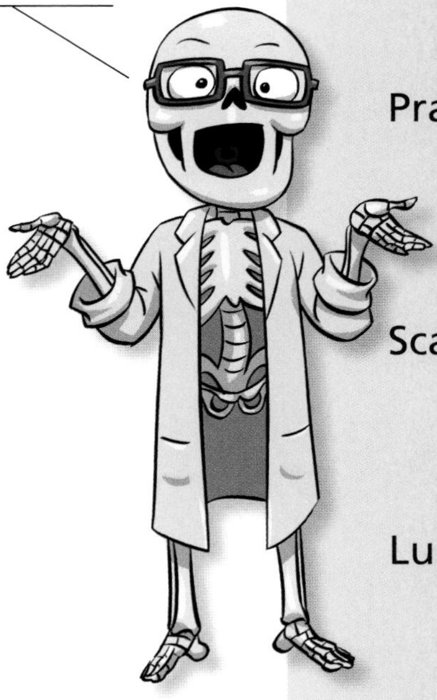

Scaphoid

Lunate

Triquetral

Pisiform

Hamate

Capitate

Trapezoid

Trapezium

The Train

_____ _____

_____ _____

_____ _____

_____ _____

_____ _____

_____ _____

_____ _____

Fun Fact:
The carpals are one of the most complex joint structures in the human body.

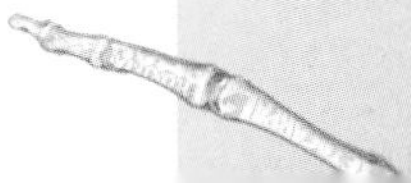

75

Activity: Carpals

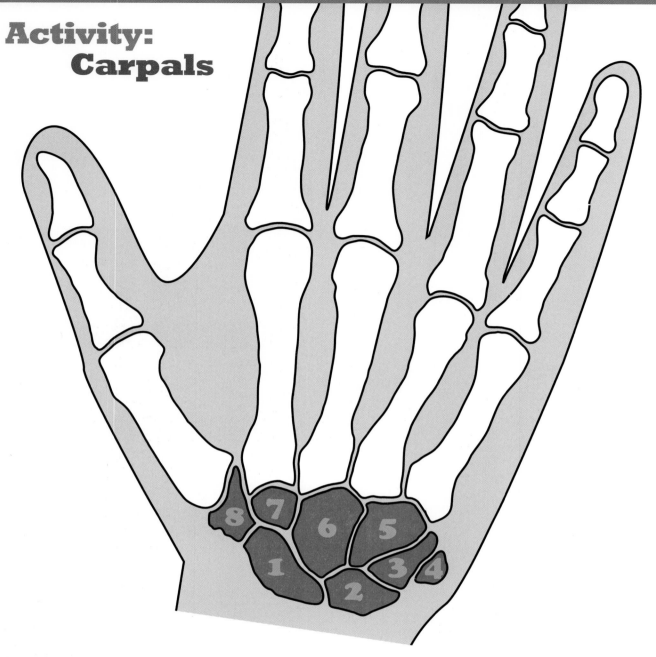

Can you write the names of all 8 carpal bones?

Proximals

1 _____

2 _____

3 _____

4 _____

Distals

5 _____

6 _____

7 _____

8 _____

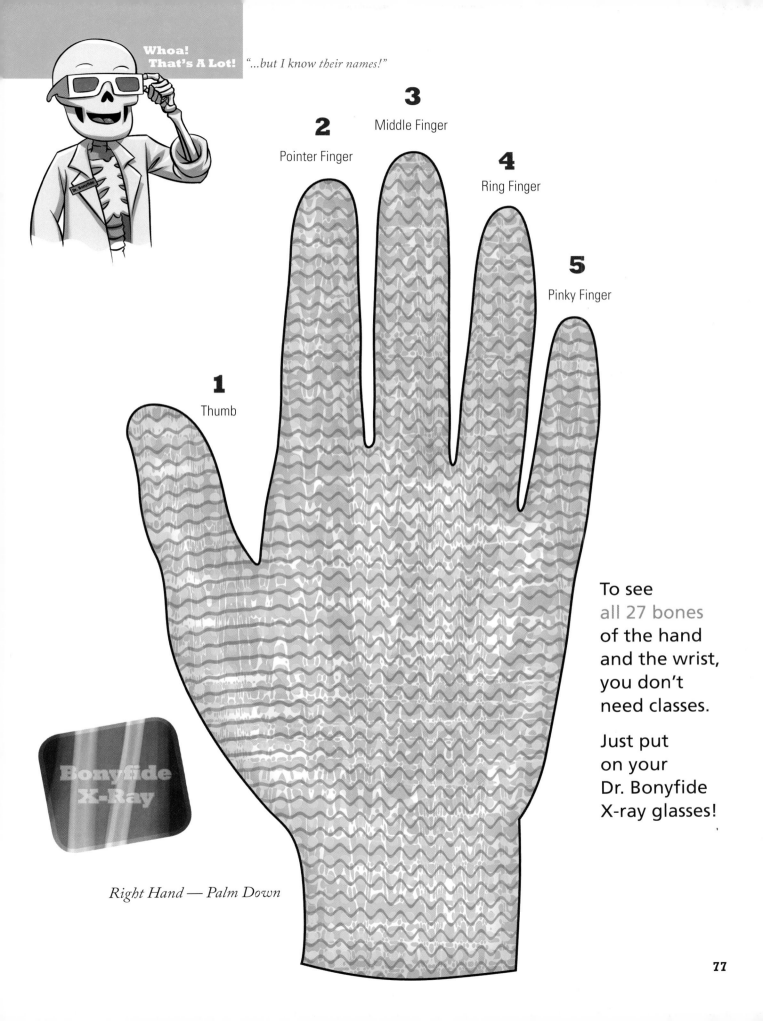

3
Middle Finger

2
Pointer Finger

4
Ring Finger

5
Pinky Finger

1
Thumb

To see all 27 bones of the hand and the wrist, you don't need classes.

Just put on your Dr. Bonyfide X-ray glasses!

Bonyfide X-Ray

Right Hand — Palm Down

Activity: Word Search

Bones of the Hand and Wrist

N G L M O A A I N S W K S I D
V H Y W O O B W R L D W N C I
I B S M U I Z E P A R T D F T
T B Q C Z X T R A P E Z O I D
B J Z P I S I F O R M U V Z S
C S D P R O X I M A L Z K T J
J X D Q N A P E J C H B U D C
N M E F Y Z D S C A P H O I D
E B V T R I Q U E T R A L S K
Z P P H A L A N G E S M L T Y
O S V T S T L O C M W A L A P
H O E B A P I K N Z X T C L S
Q K K P Z P D P R G M E Q Y I
Z L W M Q L U N A T E D W O R
N Q B C W E T C U C W L X Z S

CAPITATE	METACARPALS	TRAPEZIUM
DISTAL	PHALANGES	TRAPEZOID
HAMATE	PISIFORM	TRIQUETRAL
INTERMEDIATE	PROXIMAL	HOO-AH-HA
LUNATE	SCAPHOID	HA-HA-HA!

78

"Hey, that's not a bone!"

"But this is!"

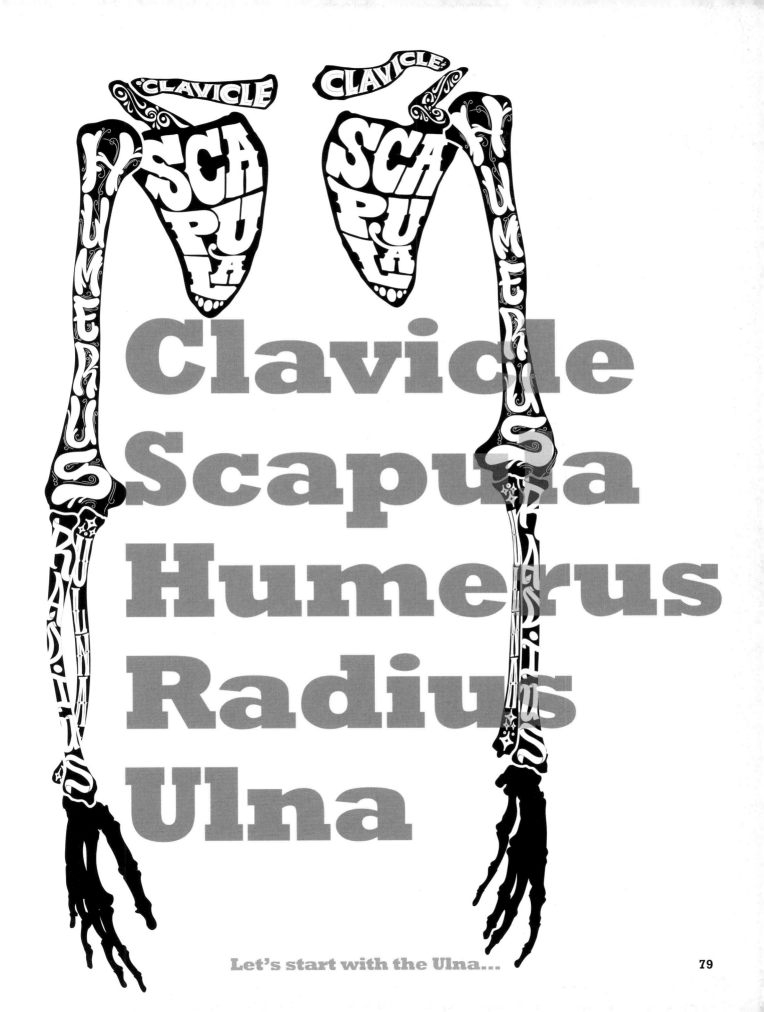

Clavicle
Scapula
Humerus
Radius
Ulna

Let's start with the Ulna…

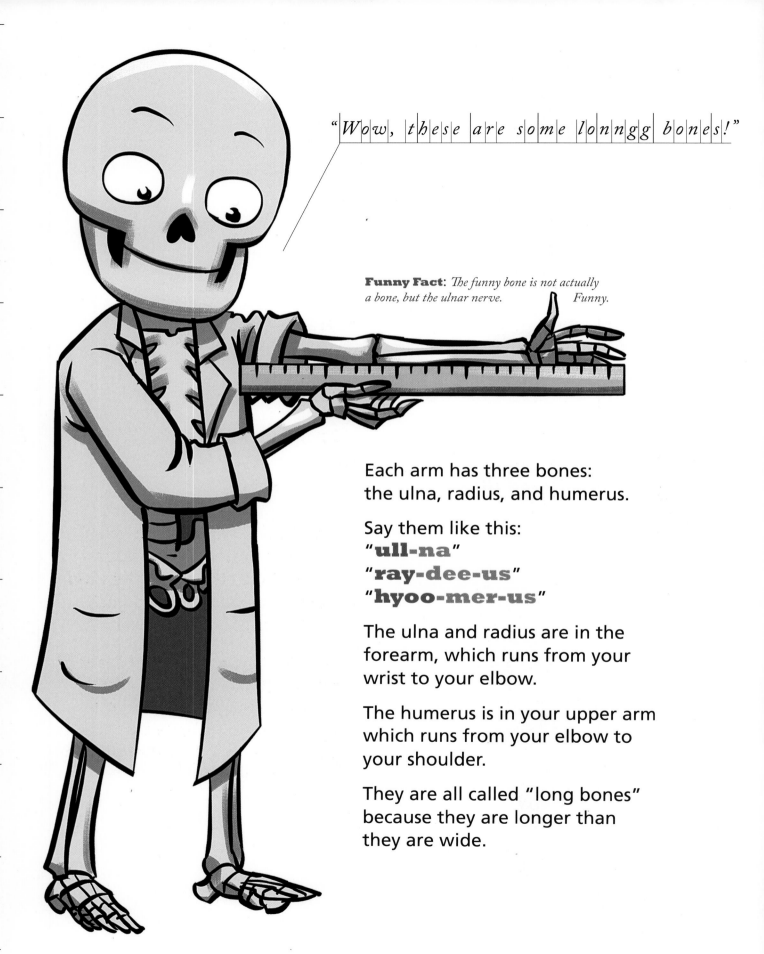

"*Wow, these are some lonngg bones!*"

Funny Fact: *The funny bone is not actually a bone, but the ulnar nerve.* *Funny.*

Each arm has three bones: the ulna, radius, and humerus.

Say them like this:
"ull-na"
"ray-dee-us"
"hyoo-mer-us"

The ulna and radius are in the forearm, which runs from your wrist to your elbow.

The humerus is in your upper arm which runs from your elbow to your shoulder.

They are all called "long bones" because they are longer than they are wide.

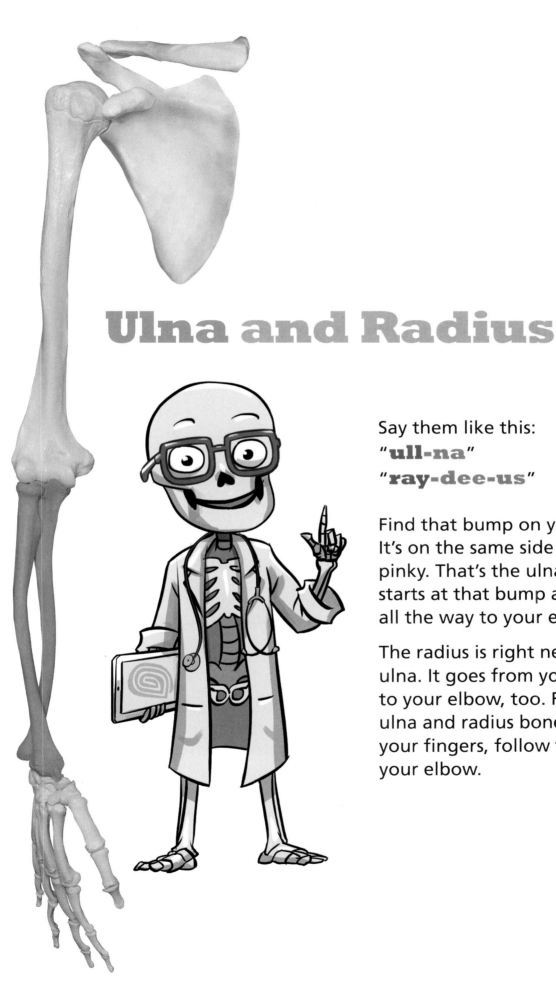

Ulna and Radius

Say them like this:
"ull-na"
"ray-dee-us"

Find that bump on your wrist. It's on the same side as your pinky. That's the ulna. The ulna starts at that bump and goes all the way to your elbow.

The radius is right next to your ulna. It goes from your wrist to your elbow, too. Feel your ulna and radius bones, and with your fingers, follow them up to your elbow.

"Dr. B., is there anything humorous about the humerus bone?"

Humerus

Say it like this: **"hyoo-mer-us"**

The bone of the upper arm is the humerus. It's the bone that starts at the elbow and fits right into the shoulder.

Bend your arm. That point is your elbow. It's the lower end of your humerus bone.

"Not at all, Pinky. Let me explain..."

The humerus bone is what is known as the upper part of your arm. It helps you when throwing and batting and rowing, along with the bottom forearm.

Activity: Ulna, Radius, and Humerus

Say "ulna," "radius," and "humerus" 3 times each.
Then, write them on the lines.

Ulna

Radius

Humerus

Activity: Ulna, Radius, and Humerus

To see the ulna, radius, and humerus, you don't need classes.

Just put on your Dr. Bonyfide X-ray glasses!

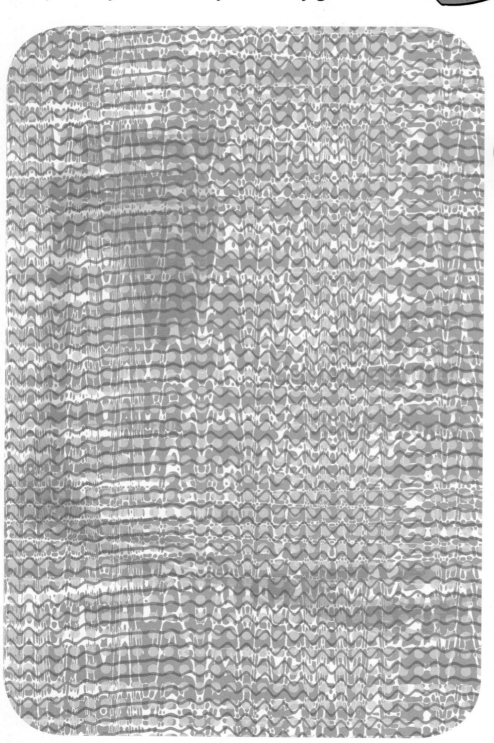

The most commonly broken bone in the forearm is the one you see broken in this X-ray.

Which bone is broken?

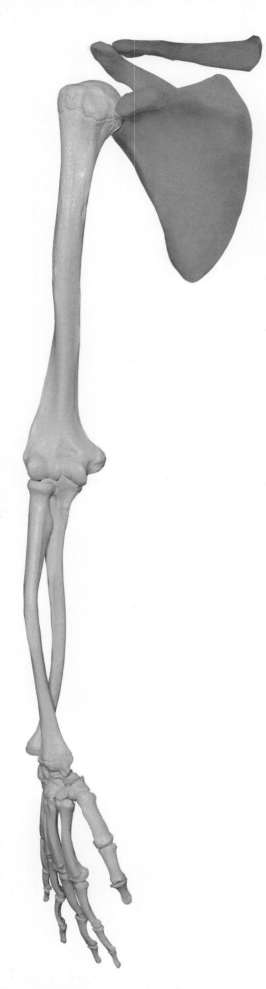

Scapula and Clavicle

The shoulder has two bones, the scapula and the clavicle.

Say them like this:
"skap-yu-la" and **"klav-i-kull"**

The scapula is also called the "shoulder blade." Its name comes from the Greek word *skaptein*, which means "to dig," because it looks like a shovel. Reach over your shoulder and feel the shoulder blade.

The clavicle is also called the "collar bone." It sits at your collar and is the only horizontal bone in your whole skeleton. Find your clavicle at the base of your neck and follow it with your fingertips to the corner of your shoulder.

Activity: Scapula and Clavicle

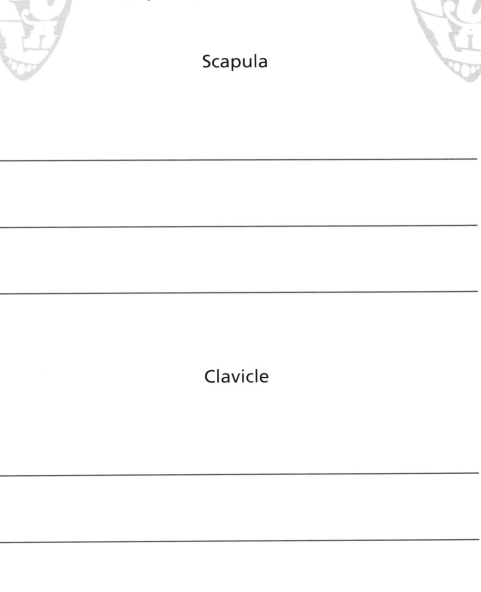

Say
"scapula" and "clavicle"
3 times each.

Then, write them on the lines.

Scapula

_____

_____

_____

Clavicle

_____

_____

_____

Activity: Scapula and Clavicle

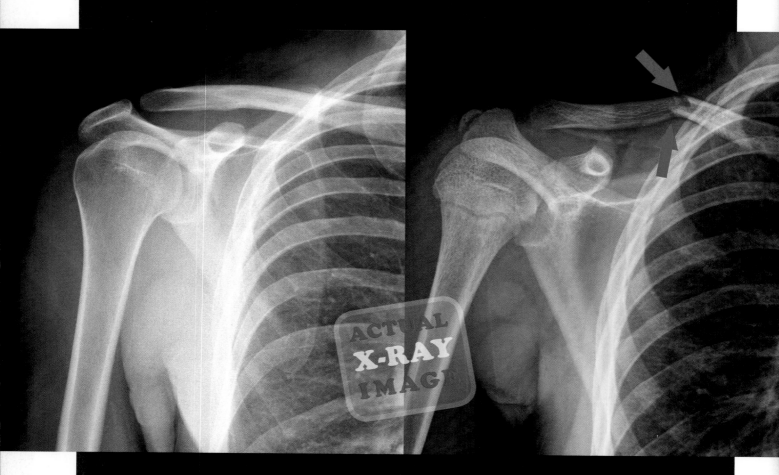

Look at these shoulder X-rays.

The left X-ray shows a normal shoulder and the right X-ray shows a broken bone.

Which bone is broken?

Activity: Scapula and Clavicle

To see the scapula and clavicle, you don't need classes.

Just put on your Dr. Bonyfide X-ray glasses!

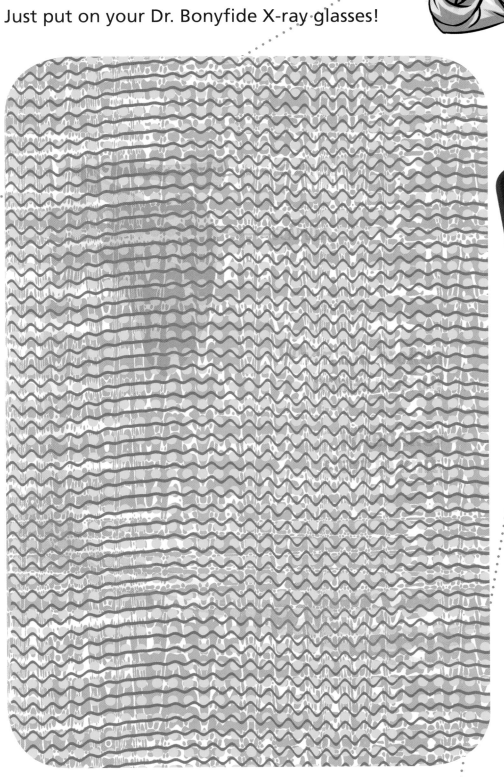

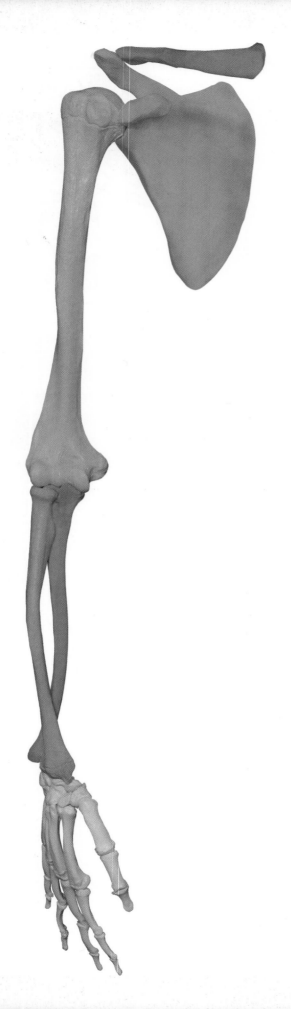

Activity: Arm and Shoulder Bones

Draw a line from the colored bone to its correct name.

Ulna

Radius

Humerus

Scapula

Clavicle

Crossword Bones
f the Hands, Arms, and Shoulders

start here...

across

4. The study of bones with Dr. Bonyfide.
5. The carpal bone located under the thumb.
9. Phalange closest to the palm.
11. The three-cornered carpal bone.
15. The eight bones of the wrist.
17. One of two bones going from wrist to elbow.
18. Means farthest from something.
19. Starts at the bump on the wrist and goes to the elbow.

down

1. The carpal bone with the smooth, rounded head.
2. From the Latin word *hamus* meaning "hook."
3. A word-trick to help you remember.
6. These five bones are found in your palm.
7. The anatomical name for finger bones.
8. Carpal bone shaped like the crescent moon.
10. This phalange makes your fingers long.

11. From the Latin word *trapezion* meaning "little table."
12. Carpal bone shaped like a hollow shell or boat.
13. The smallest carpal bone.
14. This bone sits between the shoulder and elbow.
15. Known as the collarbone.
16. Shoulder bone that looks like a shovel blade.

SEE ANSWER KEY AT THE BACK OF THE BOOK?

You Did It!

Well done, Bonyfide Buddies!
What dedication you've shown.
You're an extremities expert,
and your mind, it has grown.

You've learned 64 bones
of the structure inside.
Your knowledge has power.
CONGRATS, you're Bonyfide!

Wait! Before you head out,
there's more knowledge to gain.
It's some fun Bone-Us Knowledge
to tickle your brain.

And you've earned one more surprise.
Check the back of this book.
It's your official certificate.
Go on, take a look!

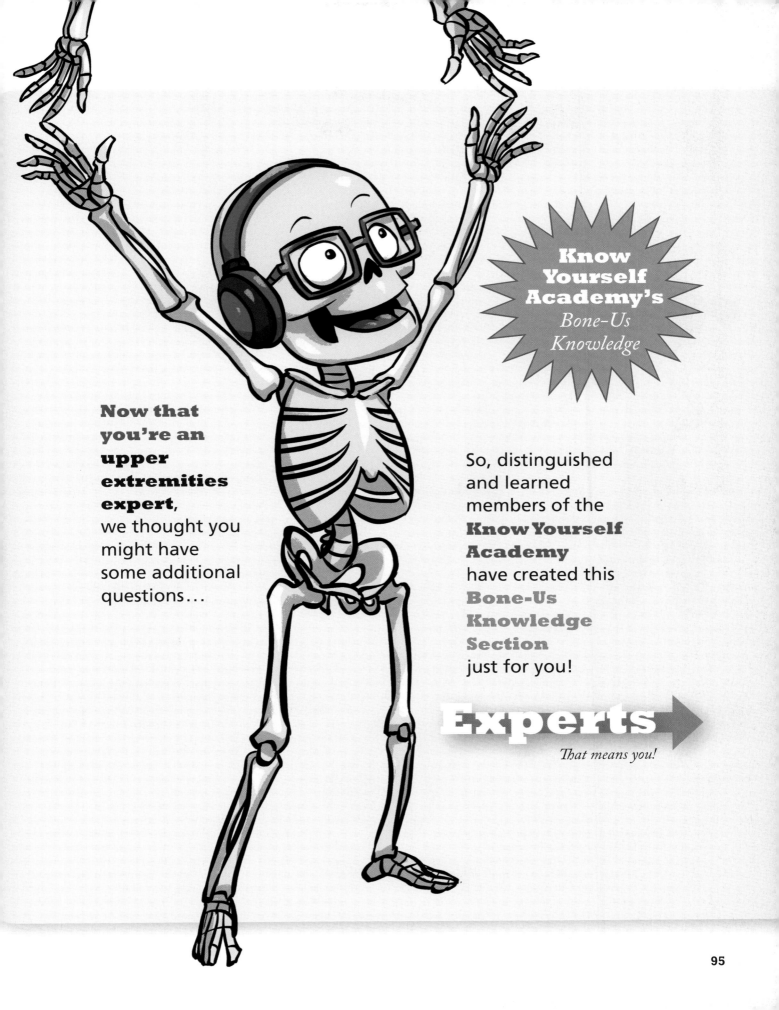

Now that you're an upper extremities expert, we thought you might have some additional questions…

Know Yourself Academy's *Bone-Us Knowledge*

So, distinguished and learned members of the **Know Yourself Academy** have created this **Bone-Us Knowledge Section** just for you!

Experts ➤

That means you!

Bone Composition

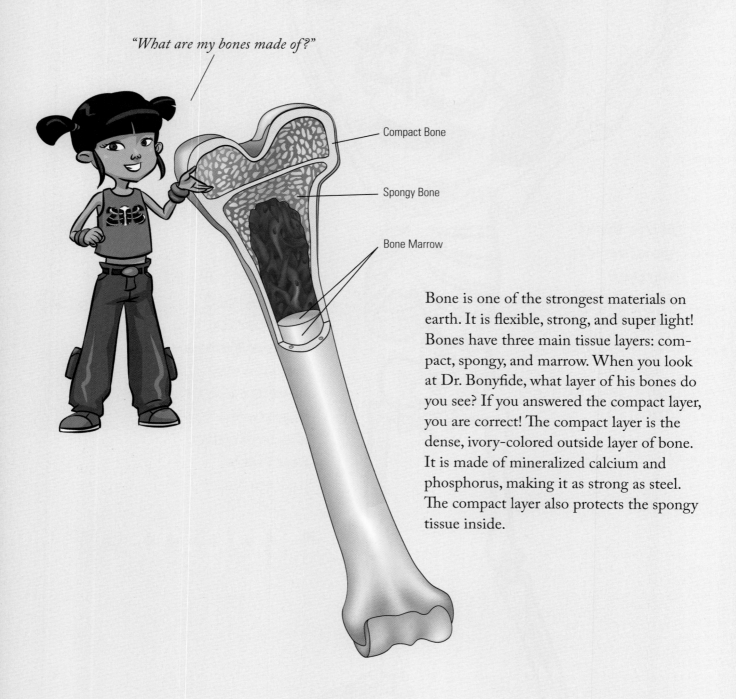

"What are my bones made of?"

Compact Bone

Spongy Bone

Bone Marrow

Bone is one of the strongest materials on earth. It is flexible, strong, and super light! Bones have three main tissue layers: compact, spongy, and marrow. When you look at Dr. Bonyfide, what layer of his bones do you see? If you answered the compact layer, you are correct! The compact layer is the dense, ivory-colored outside layer of bone. It is made of mineralized calcium and phosphorus, making it as strong as steel. The compact layer also protects the spongy tissue inside.

Fun Fact: *Bone is about four times lighter than steel.*

Bone Composition

The layer of Dr. Bonyfide's bones that you don't see is the spongy layer. It sort of looks like a kitchen sponge, doesn't it? Its spongy construction makes it flexible and lightweight.

Spongy bone is located in the backbones, next to the joints, and in the ends of long bones, like your humerus. The spongy bone protects the innermost part of the bone, called the marrow.

Bone Marrow

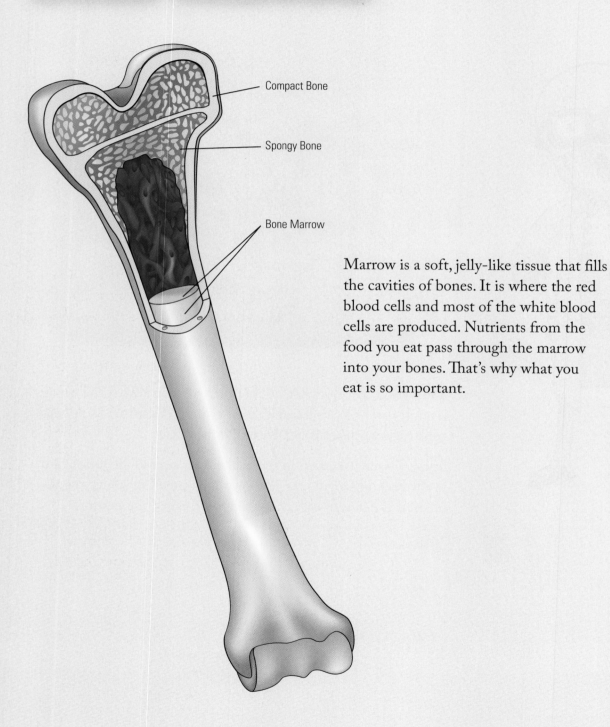

Compact Bone

Spongy Bone

Bone Marrow

Marrow is a soft, jelly-like tissue that fills the cavities of bones. It is where the red blood cells and most of the white blood cells are produced. Nutrients from the food you eat pass through the marrow into your bones. That's why what you eat is so important.

Fun Fact: *Did you know that your bones will stop growing when you are about 25 years old?*

Joints

"Now I know what my bones are made of, but how do they move?"

"Joints, ligaments, and tendons all help your bones move. First, let's look at joints."

Do you dance, skate, play a sport or an instrument? Well, you might wonder how you are able to bend your arms and legs without much effort and make such great moves.

The answer lies in your joints. Joints help your bones move in different directions. Joints are places where two bones join together. Without them, our fingers could not play the piano, our wrist could not maneuver a tennis racket, and our arms could not reach for the highest pomegranate on the tree!

There are six types of joints in the human body. Let's explore each one and find out where they are located.

Fun Fact: *When you make a fist with your hand, the bones that stick out are called knuckles.*

Joints

"What kind of joint is my wrist?"

"Move it back and forth, and side to side. That's an ellipsoidal joint!"

Ellipsoidal Joint

Say it like this: *"il-lip-**soy**-dul"*

Some joints, like those in your fingers and wrist, are ellipsoidal joints. The ellipsoidal joint is where the oval-shaped end of one bone fits into the cup-shaped end of another bone. It allows back-and-forth and side-to-side movement.

Find the ellipsoidal joints in your fingers, then your wrist. Which ways do they move?

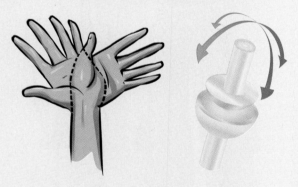

Hinge Joint

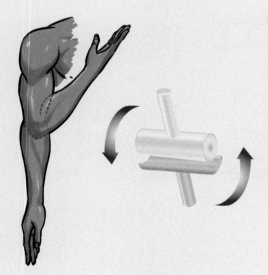

The hinge joint found in your elbow helps your arm bend and straighten.

Find it and watch how it bends. Does it open and close like a door? (Doors have hinges, too!)

Hinge joints are also found in the ankle and knee.

Joints

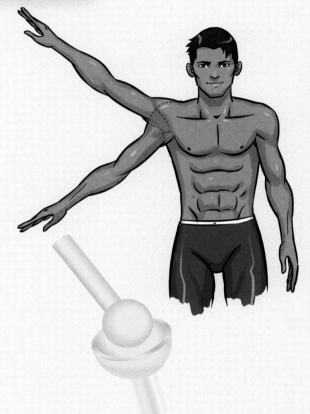

Ball-and-Socket Joint

Your ball-and-socket joints are the most mobile joints in your body. They allow you to move in many different directions. Think of a dancer, a hockey player, a figure skater, and a gymnast. The ball-and-socket joints help them move the way they do. In the ball-and-socket joint, one bone has a "ball" (a rounded end) and the other bone has a "socket" (a hollowed-out end). Your shoulder and your hip are ball-and-socket joints.

Let's experiment with the kinds of movements you can make with your shoulder and hip joints. Can you bend, flex, and move your arms and legs in different directions? If you can, you are using your ball-and-socket joints!

Pivot Joint

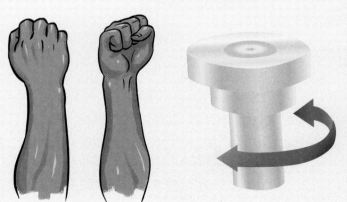

Quick! Look to your right! Look to your left! Put your palms up! Put your palms down! Congratulations – you just used your pivot joints! They are located in your neck and your wrists. In these pivot joints, a peg-shaped bone rotates inside a ring-shaped bone. A pivot joint helps a part of your body rotate.

Joints

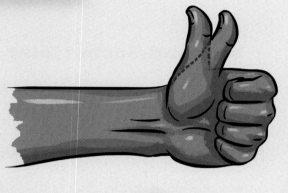

Saddle Joint

Dr. Bonyfide says, "Thumbs up if you have learned a lot about your joints so far!" If you just gave a thumbs up, then you used a very unique joint in your body—the saddle joint at the base of your thumb. It's called a saddle joint because the two bones that connect to make it have saddle-shaped ends.

The saddle joint allows your thumb to rock back and forth and side to side. It allows your thumb to cross over the palm of the hand and touch the finger pads opposite to it. We call this an opposable thumb. The saddle joint makes this movement possible.

Plane Joint

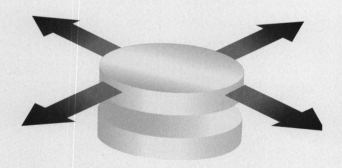

Waving your hand side to side while holding your forearm steady is one way of using a plane joint in your body. A plane joint is when the flat surfaces of two bones meet and glide against one another. For that reason they are sometimes called gliding joints. They are found in your wrists and ankles.

Cartilage, Ligaments, Tendons

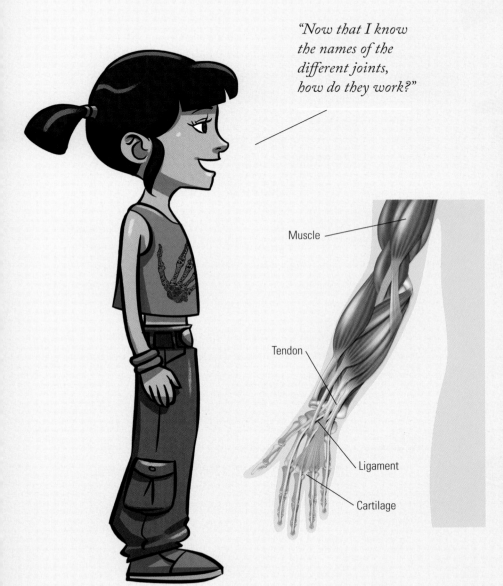

"Now that I know the names of the different joints, how do they work?"

Muscle

Tendon

Ligament

Cartilage

Joints need some special helpers to move your bones. Cartilage, ligaments, and tendons do this job.

Cartilage acts like a soft cushion and keeps the bones from scraping against each other. Your ears and nose are flexible because they are made of cartilage. That's why you can bend them.

Ligaments and tendons are called connective tissue because they connect two bones or a muscle and a bone. They are strong and stretchy like rubber bands. Ligaments connect bones with other bones so they stay in the right place. Tendons securely connect muscles to bones so the muscles don't slip off.

Bone Nutrition

If your bones could talk, this is what they would say, "Feed me delicious and nutritious foods to help me stay strong and dense!" What foods do you think would appear on a menu for healthy bones? Would it include spinach or mushrooms? Milk or eggs? Pumpkin seeds, brown rice, or berries? Actually, it would include all of these foods! Your bones need foods rich in the minerals and vitamins that keep them strong—like calcium, magnesium, and Vitamin D.

The best source of Vitamin D comes from sunshine. That's why it's important to play outside.

Calcium is the most important mineral for your bones. Dark green leafy vegetables (spinach, Swiss chard, kale), dairy products (milk, yogurt, cheese), and salmon are rich in calcium—and delicious, too!

Vitamin D and magnesium help your body absorb and use calcium, so you need them along with calcium! Pumpkin seeds, brown rice, and beans have lots of magnesium. Eating egg yolks, mushrooms, and salmon can give your bones the Vitamin D they need.

If you want to have strong bones when you are an adult, it is important to build them now by eating healthy foods.

Exercise

"Carrying heavy packages also works!"

Exercise also helps create mineral-dense bones.

Beginning to exercise at an early age will help you form habits that will be good for your bones. Exercise makes us strong, well-balanced, and coordinated, which can mean fewer bone fractures.

The best exercises work your bones and muscles against gravity. These are called weight-bearing exercises. Some examples are walking up stairs, hiking, playing tennis, and lifting weights.

Bone Density Quiz

Read the questions and fill in the blanks with the correct answers.

1. Weight-bearing exercises help build the _____- density of your bones.
   [**mineral, protein, carbohydrate**].

2. The most important mineral for bone density is _____
   [**calcium, potassium, sodium**].

3. [**Popcorn, Dark green leafy vegetables, Wheat toast**]
   _____ has/have lots of calcium.

4. [**Salmon, Orange juice, Coconut**] _____

   has lots of Vitamin D.

5. Strong, healthy bones are mineral-_____ [**loss, hard, dense**].

6. [**Hiking, Bicycling, Walking up stairs**] _____

   are examples of weight-bearing exercises.

Decode These Bones

Decipher the hidden messages below.
Use your Dr. Bonyfide X-ray glasses to see the answers.

A	B	C	D	E	F	G	H	I	J	K	L	M	N	O	P	Q	R	S	T	U	V	W	X	Y	Z
26	23	2	8	9	15	11	25	13	1	14	24	17	6	3	18	22	7	21	5	16	19	10	20	12	4

P\
18 25 26 24 26 6 11 9 21   15 3 7 17   12 3 16 7   15 13 6 11 9 7 21

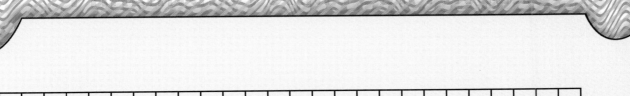

A	B	C	D	E	F	G	H	I	J	K	L	M	N	O	P	Q	R	S	T	U	V	W	X	Y	Z
18	15	3	26	8	19	10	14	16	5	9	1	22	23	13	24	20	7	2	12	21	6	11	25	4	17

K\
9 23 13 11   4 13 21 7   2 8 1 19   19 8 8 1   12 14 8   24 13 11 8 7

Hidden Message Quiz

Decipher the hidden messages below.
Use your Dr. Bonyfide X-ray glasses to see the answers.

A	B	C	D	E	F	G	H	I	J	K	L	M	N	O	P	Q	R	S	T	U	V	W	X	Y	Z
L	T	K	R	V	D	W	M	P	A	B	F	E	I	S	X	O	H	N	C	U	Z	G	J	Y	Q

M

E V C L K L H X L F   D P Z V

A	B	C	D	E	F	G	H	I	J	K	L	M	N	O	P	Q	R	S	T	U	V	W	X	Y	Z
Σ	Ξ	Δ	E	ρ	T	δ	λ	Ω	Φ	Θ	A	χ	o	N	Γ	H	ψ	Y	π	B	I	Π	K	Z	M

S

Y N   A N O δ   π N   Γ Ω O Θ Z

Answer Key

Page 13
Phalanges form your **fingers**. Each finger has **three**. Except for the **thumb**. With just **two** as you can see.

Page 16
How many phalanges are in one hand? 14

Page 22
Intermediate phalanges make your fingers **long**. Conductors use long **fingers** to orchestrate a song. Or to get the Bonyfide **choir** to sing along.

Page 23
1. One 2. Four 3. Thumb 4. None

Page 27
proximal phalange

Page 30
1. There are five **proximal** phalanges close to your palm.
2. There are four **intermediate** phalanges in the middle of your fingers.
3. There are five **distal** phalanges at the tips of your fingers.
4. How many phalanges are in one hand? **14**

Page 31
Distal at the tips.
Intermediate in the middle.
Proximal at the base.

Page 39
How many bones have you drawn? 19

Page 48
Scaphoid, Lunate, Triquetral, Pisiform

Page 51
scaphoid

Page 59
(clockwise)
Scaphoid, Lunate, Pisiform, Triquetral

Page 72
(clockwise)
Hamate, Capitate, Trapezium, Trapezoid

Page 76
1. Scaphoid 2. Lunate 3. Triquetral
4. Pisiform 5. Hamate 6. Capitate
7. Trapezoid 8. Trapezium

Page 78
Solution for Word Search on next page.

Page 82
ulna

Page 90
clavicle or collarbone

Page 93
Solution for Crossword on next page.

Page 106
1. Weight-bearing exercises help build the **mineral**-density of your bones.
2. The most important mineral for bone density is **calcium**.
3. **Dark green leafy vegetables** have lots of calcium.
4. **Salmon** has lots of Vitamin D.
5. Strong, healthy bones are mineral-**dense**.
6. **Hiking** and **walking up stairs** are examples of weight-bearing exercises.

Answer Key

Page 78:

Word Search Solution

WORD (*Over, Down, Direction*)

CAPITATE (10, 15, NW)

DISTAL (14, 7, S)

HAMATE (12, 8, S)

INTERMEDIATE (14, 1, SW)

LUNATE (6, 14, E)

METACARPALS (10, 11, N)

PHALANGES (3, 10, E)

PISIFORM (4, 5, E)

PROXIMAL (4, 6, E)

SCAPHOID (8, 8, E)

TRAPEZIUM (12, 3, W)

TRAPEZOID (7, 4, E)

TRIQUETRAL (4, 9, E)

Page 93:
Crossword Solution
Bones of the Hands, Arms, and Shoulders

Glossary

American Manual Alphabet: A form of fingerspelling used by the deaf community in the United States and in English-speaking parts of Canada. It is used along with the American Sign Language vocabulary.

Boneology: The study of bones with Dr. Bonyfide. When you study bones in medical school it is called osteology.

Bonyfide Buddy: Anyone who takes the journey with Dr. Bonyfide to "Know Yourself" through a study of the bones.

Capitate: This word derives from the Latin capitātus, meaning "head." One of eight carpal bones of the wrist located in the distal row. It is a head-shaped bone situated at the base of metacarpal #3 between the hamate and the trapezoid.

Carpals: The eight bones of the wrist. They are named scaphoid, lunate, triquetral, pisiform, hamate, capitate, trapezoid, and trapezium.

Clavicle: Either of two slender, horizontal bones across the front of the neck which are part of the shoulder. Commonly called the collarbone.

Decipher: To discover the meaning of a secret message by use of a key.

Digit: Digit is another word for a finger or toe. There are five digits on each hand and five digits on each foot.

Distal: Situated away from the point of origin or attachment.

Distal Carpals: The group of four carpals located farthest from your arm, but closest to the palm. They are named scaphoid, lunate, triquetral, and pisiform.

Distal Phalanges: The bones that are located in the tips of your fingers. There are five distal phalanges in each hand.

Etymology: The study of the history of words, where they come from, and how they change over time.

Fingerspelling: See American Manual Alphabet.

Hamate: This word derives from the Latin hamus, meaning "hook." The hamate is one of the eight carpal bones of the wrist located in the distal row. It is a hook-shaped bone situated at the base of metacarpal #5 next to the capitate.

Hand: The part of the human body at the end of your arm that can grasp and hold things.

Humerus: The long bone of the upper arm, extending from the elbow to the shoulder.

Index Finger: The first finger and the second digit of a human hand. It is located between the first and third digits, or between the thumb and the middle finger. It is the finger you use for pointing.

Intermediate Phalanges: The bones in the middle of your fingers. There are four in each hand. They are located between your distal phalanges and your proximal phalanges.

Know Yourself: Modern take on the Ancient Greek aphorism "Know Thyself" which has been discussed through the ages by the world's greatest philosophers.

Lunate: This word derives from the Latin luna, which means "moon." One of the eight carpal bones of the wrist, located in proximal row. It is a crescent, moon-shaped bone situated below metacarpal #3. It sits between the scaphoid and the triquetral bones.

Metacarpals: The five bones that make up your palm.

Middle Finger: The third digit of the human hand, located between the index finger and the ring finger. It is usually the longest finger.

Osteologist: A doctor who specializes in osteology.

Osteology: The branch of anatomy that deals with the structure and function of bones.

Palm: The inner area of the hand between the base of the fingers and the wrist.

Phalange: Any one of the bones of the finger. Singular for phalanges.

Phalanges: The 14 bones of the fingers. There are three phalanges in each finger, and two phalanges in each thumb.

Pinky: The little finger, often called the pinky. The word is derived from the Dutch word pink, meaning "little finger." It is usually the smallest finger of the human hand.

Pisiform: This word derives from the Latin *pisum,* meaning "pea." One of the eight carpal bones of the wrist, located in the proximal row. It is a small pea-shaped bone situated below metacarpal #5, next to the triquetral bone.

Pointer Finger: Another name for your index finger.

Proximal: Situated near the point of origin or attachment.

Proximal Carpals:The group of four wrist bones located closest to your arm. They are named hamate, capitate, trapezoid, and trapezium.

Proximal Phalanges: The five finger bones that are closest to your palm.

Radius: One of the two long bones of the forearm. The radius is the larger of two bones of the forearm. It extends from the wrist to the elbow on the thumb side of the arm.

Ring Finger: The fourth proximal digit of the human hand. It is located between the middle finger and the little finger.

Scaphoid: This word derives from the Greek words *skaphos,* meaning "boat or hollow shell" and *eidos,* meaning "a type." One of the eight carpal bones of the wrist, located in the proximal row. The scaphoid is a boat-shaped bone situated below metacarpals #1 and #2, next to the lunate bone.

Scapula: Commonly called the shoulder blade, this flat triangular bone forms the back part of the shoulder.

Skeleton: The 206 bones forming the framework of the human body.

Thumb: The thumb is the first digit of the hand and is unique in its ability to touch the fingertips of the other four digits. The thumb makes complex movements of the hand possible.

Trapezium: This word derives from the Greek *trapézion,* meaning "little table." One of the eight carpal bones of the wrist, located in the distal row. It is a table-shaped bone situated below metacarpal #1 next to the trapezoid carpal bone.

Trapezoid: This word derives from the Greek *trapézion,* meaning "little table." One of the eight carpal bones of the wrist located in the distal row. It is a table-shaped bone situated below metacarpals #1 and #2 between the trapezium and capitate bones.

Triquetral: This word derives from the Latin *triquetrus,* meaning "three-cornered." One of the eight carpal bones of the wrist located in the proximal row. It is a three-cornered bone situated below metacarpals #4 and #5 between the lunate and pisiform bones.

Ulna: One of the two long bones of the forearm. It extends from the wrist to the elbow on the pinky side of the arm.

Wrist: The joint between the hand and the forearm. There are eight carpal bones that articulate together to form the wrist. These eight bones form the most complex joint in the human body.

X-ray: X-ray technology allows doctors to see through your skin and look inside your body.

X-ray Glasses: A totally cool way to look at pictures of bones under the skin. Use your Dr. Bonyfide glasses throughout this book.

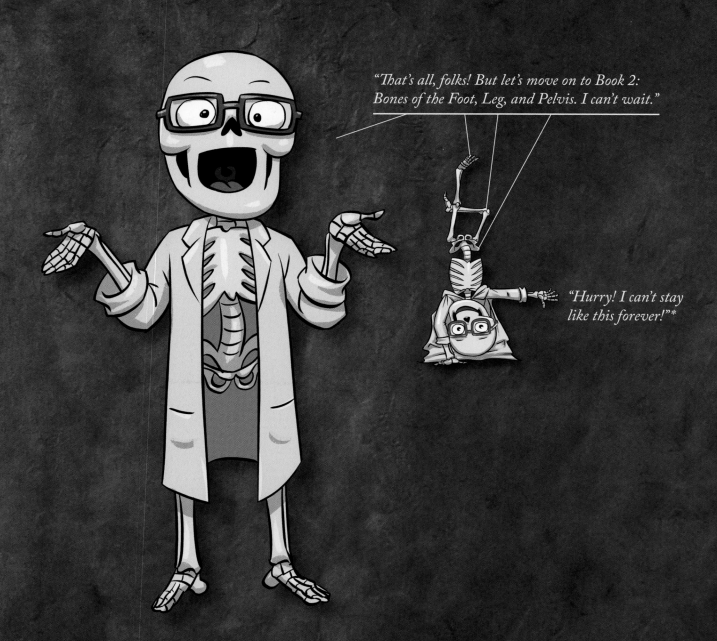

"That's all, folks! But let's move on to Book 2: Bones of the Foot, Leg, and Pelvis. I can't wait."

"Hurry! I can't stay like this forever!"*

*"and those lines aren't holding me up, either!"

Contributors

Linda Balfour
Dwight Davis
Emily Del Conte
Dale Dickerson
Helen Heaslip
Lidie Howes
Madeline Howes
Nancy Howes
Dr. Timothy Howes
Zhi Howes
Mitchell Lum
Anne MacKenzie
Whitney Noble
Vanessa Norton
Bonnie O'Connell
Kimberly Stinson Serrano
Sarah Spinner
Joanie Thompson
Parents of the 2012-2013
    Second Grade at Sacred Heart
    Schools, Atherton, CA

Credits

Art Director: Molly Rubin
Illustration Credits:
abcteach.com
Tony DiPietro
DiscoveryEducation.com
Helmi Himawan
Jovan Obradovic
Puliatti Photographic 2014
Oke Rosgana
Roni Setiawan
Easten Tanimoto
Dave Thompson/dtstudio.com
Alila Medical Media/Shutterstock.com
Allies Interactive/Shutterstock.com
andrea crisante/Shutterstock.com
Callahan/Shutterstock.com
Crepesoles/Shutterstock.com
cybrain/Shutterstock.com
Dim Dimich/Shutterstock.com
DM7/Shutterstock.com
eAlisa/Shutterstock.com
Givaga/Shutterstock.com
itsmejust/Shutterstock.com
James Steidl/Shutterstock.com
KennyK/Shutterstock.com
Kun Kunko/Shutterstock.com
Laili/Shutterstock.com
Malchev/Shutterstock.com
Markus Mainka/Shutterstock.com
Oligo/Shutterstock.com
Rocket400 Studio/Shutterstock.com
Sergey Mironov/Shutterstock.com
Suzanne Tucker/Shutterstock.com
wonderisland/Shutterstock.com
Yoko Design/Shutterstock.com
Louis Philippe Lessard/Wikimedia Commons

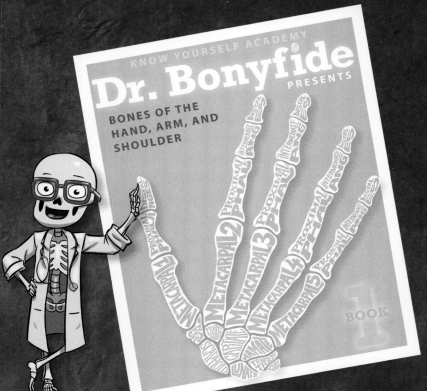
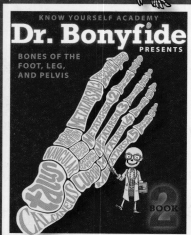
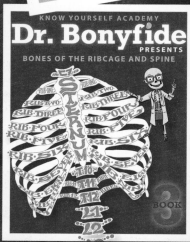
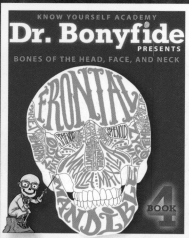